RADICAL
GRATITUDE

Also by Ellen Vaughn

The God Who Hung on the Cross
(with Dois I. Rosser Jr.)

ELLEN VAUGHN

DISCOVERING *JOY*

THROUGH *EVERYDAY*

THANKFULNESS

RADICAL GRATITUDE

ZONDERVAN™

GRAND RAPIDS, MICHIGAN 49530 USA

ZONDERVAN™

Radical Gratitude
Copyright © 2005 by Ellen Santilli Vaughn

Requests for information should be addressed to:

Zondervan, Grand Rapids, Michigan 49530

Cataloging-in-Publication Data available from the Library of Congress.

ISBN-10: 0-310-25749-2

ISBN-13: 978-0-310-25749-3

This edition printed on acid-free paper.

Published in association with Wolgemuth & Associates, Inc.

Interior design by Beth Shagene

Printed in the United States of America

05 06 07 08 09 10 11 12 /❖ DCI/ 10 9 8 7 6 5 4 3 2 1

With a heart full of love and gratitude
I remember
Mildred Coursey Miller Santilli
1913–2002

CONTENTS

FOREWORD

When I met Ellen Vaughn in 1980, she was fresh out of graduate school. It was five years since I'd been released from prison, four years into Prison Fellowship's ministry. When Ellen came to work for me, we clicked; our marvelous working relationship was based on a common world view, similar gut reactions to life's issues and incongruities, and a "Far Side" sense of humor. We worked together for more than twenty years, collaborating on books, articles, and other writing projects.

Our relationship had many facets. Though we were colleagues in ministry, of course, there was also a father-daughter, mentoring dynamic. Over the years, I've watched Ellen develop into a tremendous communicator; she has honed her writing and speaking skills with determination and excellence. I'd like to think that I taught her, at least in the beginning days; but in more recent times, she's been teaching me.

God gifted Ellen with an unusually keen ability to tell stories—to paint on paper the poignant reality of life's everyday beauties and ironies, as well as the high drama of unusual tales. We have always shared a strong belief that stories well told can communicate truth in a way that didactic "telling" does not, bypassing intellectual barriers to penetrate straight to the heart. Jesus told parables: earthly stories with a heavenly point. I firmly believe the best writing does the same.

No one tells stories better than Ellen Vaughn, and *Radical Gratitude* is vintage Vaughn, beautifully written, fun, full of stories both large and small. You'll laugh, cry, and be constantly caught by surprise; *Radical Gratitude* is incredibly moving. It will provide pastors with tremendous sermon illustrations; for the rest of us, it's a book to share with friends, regardless of their spiritual perspective. It doesn't use religious jargon. It's accessible and winsome, wooing readers with the scent of God's love and grace. And it's not canned; I know Ellen well enough to know that what she writes is straight from the heart, that she has experienced the very things she writes about, which is what gives this book such conviction and power.

Because of this, *Radical Gratitude* will touch you regardless of where you are on your spiritual pilgrimage—a "seeker," new believer, or one who has been on the journey for a long time. One executive pastor who has spent forty years in ministry and recently experienced a period of trials wrote that this book "touched a very tender nerve for me. I think that the one element I had [lost] in the last few years is a heartfelt sense of thankfulness to God. I know He is sovereign in all our affairs, but I confess that it has been very difficult to be thankful for the place I am in now. So the book was very convicting—because I think it speaks truth, but it also spoke to my heart, because it was far more anecdotal than preachy."

I also believe there are few topics more important than gratitude to God. If God loves us so much that He gave His only Son to die on the cross, what is the only possible response? Gratitude. Every time I hear the word grace, I am reminded that I must live a life, every day, which reflects my gratitude to God. Few authors have dealt with the subject, certainly not in the very practical way that Ellen does in this book. Properly understood, the daily practice of thankfulness to God is a transforming tool of divine proportions. As Ellen says, real renewal beats in the pulse of a purposely grateful human heart. Toward that end, I pray that God will use this book to refresh and fire you up. Reading it is a pure pleasure. Living its truths can be life-changing.

CHARLES W. COLSON

WITH GRATITUDE

Writing a "with gratitude" page for a book on gratitude feels oddly daunting. I can't adequately express my deep thanks to those who have so graciously helped make this book possible. But I will try—for I am truly grateful.

My mother-in-law, Norma Vaughn (Saint Norma), traveled from North Carolina to Virginia several times to run domestic life in VaughnWorld while I went away to quiet places for concentrated writing interludes. Andi Brindley and Jim and Laura Warren graciously provided their beach homes as those places of quiet. Sherri Salamone, friend and school carpool buddy, jumped in to help whenever I needed to jiggle and juggle our children's schedules. A team of friends read the manuscript, or pieces of it, and graciously gave reactions, insights, and ideas: Cynthia Earley, Craig Falwell, Paula Corder, Steve Smallman, John Hutchinson, Ellie Lofaro, Jerry Leachman, Phil Callaway, Patti Bryce, Chuck and Patty Colson, Gail Harwood, and Gloria Hawley. I appreciate the prayer support of my sisters and brothers at McLean Presbyterian Church. And I am indebted to all the friends—old and new—who shared their stories of God's grace with me, so I could highlight them in this book.

I deeply appreciate my agent, Robert Wolgemuth, for his friendship and professional proficiency, not to mention his relentless good taste. I'm very grateful for John Sloan, for his creative camaraderie

11

and for caring so passionately about ideas and words, and to Bob Hudson, for his editing expertise. And I salute the rest of the Zondervan editorial, marketing, and sales groups; it is a rich pleasure to work with such a great and committed team.

I am immensely grateful to God for Emily, Haley, Walker, and Lee Vaughn, who graciously demonstrate a *Semper Gumby* attitude toward my writing schedule, and so enthusiastically cheer me onward. My husband and children are incredible gifts of grace: I will never get over the fact that God gave them to me, and me to them.

Thank You.

ELLEN VAUGHN
NOVEMBER 25, 2004

PART ONE

GRATITUDE'S SURPRISES

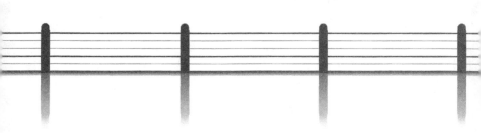

CHAPTER ONE

DEATH
AS THE DOORWAY

It was the day I had dreaded all my life. It didn't matter that I was an alleged adult with children of my own. I just wasn't ready for my mother to die.

Standing by her bed I became a small girl again, staring at the familiar shape of my mom's still hand, weeping and wanting only to hold it, warm once more.

I did not know where the day of dread would lead. To my wonder, it opened the door to a flood of fresh grace. Riding it, I've been upended, soaked, carried far downstream . . . and lifted, always lifted, by the buoyant gift of a grateful heart.

That bequest, it seems, was my mother's parting surprise.

I too had been a surprise. Mom had me at age forty-three, back in a time when middle-aged mothers weren't the norm. She had seriously spaced her children—I had siblings ten, twenty, and twenty-five years older. When I was little, my parents were my grandparents. At age ten I earnestly made my mom promise to live until she was eighty. That seemed impossibly far away, and Jesus would certainly return before then anyway.

He didn't.

But over the years, more than I realized, I learned about Him from the depth and breadth of my mother's bond. Her love was secure . . . not based on who I was or what I did, but on who she was.

I thought of her today. Two birds wheeled in flight at the edge of the woods beyond our backyard. They were synchronized, wingtip to wingtip. Then one diverged and veered off sharply. I could not see where it went. The other continued alone.

Then, unexpectedly, came the tears. Why? My mother lived a long, full life. Her death was neither premature nor unexpected. I'm at peace with that.

But peace and loss are not mutually exclusive. Despite the assurance that I'll see her again, I grieve. Her loss kaleidoscopes, multiplying through whatever prism I regard it. It telescopes, moving in and out like a zoom lens focusing on *all* the loss I feel. Past and future combine in the present: that diverging bird just now represents not only my mother and others who have gone before, but my husband, friends, children—all those I'll ever lose, one way or another. They'll drop suddenly from our bobbing flight, and I must continue alone.

Mildred Miller was born in 1913 in her parents' home in the valley of Virginia, one of nine durable children born in twelve years to John and Helen Miller. In spite of their perfectly respectable proper names, their dad called them Philip, Punker, Dutch, Puss, Cabbage, Jake, Beaner, Miss Moon, and Mouser.

To hear my mom tell it—which may not be the way it happened—she was an unusually gorgeous, intelligent, insightful, and whimsical child with short blond hair and hazel eyes. She walked on three miles of narrow dirt roads to school each day. Occasionally a car—one of those new Model T Fords—would pass Mildred and her sisters as they trudged along.

When she was twelve, she and her sisters found smooth stones and dammed the creek on the back of their property. Three days later, when the resulting pool was deep and cold, the Church of the Brethren minister arrived and dunked them all. Mildred was baptized in the name of the Father, the Son, and the Holy Ghost.

Over the years, her faith grew quietly, a steady flame within. She loved stories of brave missionaries bringing the Gospel to

China or Vietnam or India or the Ivory Coast. She prayed faithfully and tithed from her grocery money to advance their cause. She taught Sunday school, met with young women whose marriages were troubled, made curtains, dresses, and quilts, and raised her family.

Her own mother had been a domestically challenged adventurer. In spite of her nine children, she longed for the open road—and often took it. Mom's response was to become a woman who created security wherever she was; her children's roots could grow deep and strong. Home was sun-warmed laundry fresh off the line and roast beef with rich gravy, marigolds and ripe tomatoes on the vine, new neighbors at the dinner table and furloughed missionaries sleeping in our spare beds.

When I was young, she packed my lunch for school each day. Sometimes, wondering if I was paying attention to details, she would take a bite out of it. There I was, a big-eyed, dark-haired, unsuspecting child innocently unwrapping waxed paper in the elementary school lunchroom. I'd find tuna salad or ham and cheese, stacked neatly on good white bread, pristine except for the half-moon missing, Mom's dental surprise in an otherwise normal day. Once my sister got two pieces of bread with a chicken leg stuck between them, its tendoned knob emerging from between the crusts as if it had been trying to escape but couldn't.

We grew up wary, on the lookout for eccentric sandwiches and odd visitations like stuffed animals perched on the hearth, suddenly sporting cruise wear. It wasn't surprising that such intrusions on the ordinary sharpened my sense of the absurd and weakened my connection with convention. But what was lovely was that Mom's twisted wit also created a sense of wonder, humor, unlikely juxtapositions that whispered to me of a universe filled with the surprises of God.

Once, years ago, she had a coronary crisis. My dad bustled her to the hospital.

Dad was a retired Army colonel whose love of military order was both served and sabotaged by his obsession with all things technological. His office was a maze of jerry-rigged wires and surge protectors. Once he was sitting at a traffic light, mesmerized by the alternating time-and-temperature display on the bank sign at the corner. When the time changed to temperature, Dad obediently caromed into the intersection. The only problem was that the light was still red.

This was the man who sat, lovingly if not distractedly, by Mom's bed in intensive care. There were tubes for oxygen and other functions, IV carts and monitors that looked like television screens. One showed heart activity, the other respiration. Dad stared at them, transfixed by the squiggling images. They showed, reassuringly, that Mom's heart was beating and her lungs were breathing.

An evil idea evidently presented itself to my mother. Accordingly, she held her breath. The respiratory device flatlined, alarms went off, and Dad had to be revived himself.

In the end, he made the final journey first. After he died in 1988, she gave away his stuff, had the house rewired, and commenced widowhood, as she did all things, with an eager and orderly spirit that concealed, just barely, her strange and quirky side.

When she came to live with Lee and me and our three children many years later, her body was breaking down. Rheumatoid arthritis was having its way with her, stalking her nerve endings and tormenting her with terrible pain. She never talked about it unless she was asked. Her vision dimmed. But Haley and Walker, her grandchildren twins, would sit on her lap and read from their first-grade books. *Buried Treasure. Paths of Gold.* We found Barbies in strange places around the house, always wearing unusual outfits, sometimes carrying small picket signs. Mom dressed for dinner each evening, appearing with the anticipation of a special event. We all held hands and said grace. We did not serve sandwiches made of chicken legs.

As proof of her cheerful perversity, she loved our dog. He is a shaggy white labradoodle, a premeditated blend of Labrador and standard poodle. He is named for C. S. Lewis. After being a puppy for about five minutes, he commenced to grow as big as a pony, developing along the way a passion for ripe pears and any kind of bread. In defense we began storing sandwich bread on top of the refrigerator. Eventually, after foggily realizing that whole loaves were turning up missing, we realized that when Lewis stood on his hind legs he could pull them down.

One winter morning Mom felt unusually weak. After breakfast she returned to her room and crept back into bed. As he often did, the dog lay down with her, his long back fitted carefully next to hers, an innovative bed warmer with fur and paws.

I sat downstairs at my home office computer but soon felt too distracted to work. I was constantly waiting for the other shoe to drop, for that momentous moment that could so easily be missed. What if she died and I was sitting at my desk, trying to write? Or far worse, and far more likely, obsessively playing software Boggle?

I crept up the stairs, unsure what I would find. Had she slipped away? Was this the moment?

I stood outside her bedroom door, bracing myself. It was not latched. I started to push it open, gently.

Suddenly, the door burst open the rest of the way. The giant dog flew out of Mom's room, tail wagging, teeth shining, Rastafarian hair sticking straight out, quivering and prancing with pride and the delight of the moment.

He was wearing Mom's nightgown.

Just how did her brain work? I wondered later. What *was* the intellectual process that moved, thought by tidy thought, to arrive at the logical conclusion: *Clearly, the next right thing to do is to put my nightgown on the dog.*

Now, when I remember the day of the dancing dog in the long, pink nightgown, I see a cascade of images spiraling to decline. Soon came Mom's tumble on the carpeted stairs. I remember holding her and figuring so carefully just how I would get to the phone to call 911. Surgery, a cast, rehab: her challenge to the elderly man across the hall that she could beat him in a wheelchair race. A move to assisted living. "Here I am living with all these old people," she said one day after forgetting someone's name, which was unusual. "And now I'm starting to talk like one! Get out while you can! Save yourself! It's contagious!"

More hospitalizations. Nurses cutting off her clothes in the emergency room. Conferences with doctors; mind-numbing bureaucracies. Calls in the night when she was in such extreme pain that she was praying for death.

But the next morning was always new. "Here I've worked like a field hand all my life," she grumbled, "and I just can't seem to die well. And my mother—never worked a day, lazy as sin, and she gets to die at home, in bed, in her sleep! Peacefully! Doesn't seem fair, does it?" Then she would laugh at herself. She had never expected life to be "fair."

One afternoon I was sitting at my computer, nervous about meeting a writing deadline. Then came the sense that I should go be with her. I went. Her pain had been radiating, cruelly pervasive, and now she was on so much morphine that she had morphed to another place. I sat with her as she floated in and out, surprised at how her conscious and subconscious minds were such great friends. She saw fairies riding bright specks of dust down from the ceiling, then ladders stretching up to heaven. "They're having a party," she told me.

Dinner arrived: mysteries on a tray, hiding under covers, a magician's show. I held her hand and we said grace. I fed her six or seven bites of mashed potatoes, like an infant, as gently as she had once fed me.

"I'll be back in the morning," I told her before I had to leave. She pulled herself back from the party. "Bye, honey," she said, as she always had. "I love you."

The next day she waved broadly when she saw me, more robust. We talked as the nurses gave her a bed bath. Then, suddenly, she pitched forward like a sack of sand. Even in her most helpless moments, I had never seen her look so stripped of a certain, habitual grace.

Still, I thought it was the morphine. What did I know? It was a massive stroke to the right side of her brain.

My sister and I moved into Mom's room in assisted living and were assisted ourselves. Hospice nurses arrived and told us what we might expect. Friends brought food and flowers; others came from far away to say good-bye. We sang hymns, prayed, hugged everyone, and held Mom's hands for hours, relishing this luxury of a prepared farewell. Our calling came naturally, an unspoken understanding that we were to be midwives to her rebirth even as she had so kindly birthed us in pain long before. We slept on the sofas. Aides came and went in the watches of the night. I wore red slippers and big pajamas, drinking my weight in coffee each morning and prowling the halls at night like a comparatively young, but ever so slightly unbalanced, resident.

Then we came to the end, the final tableaux around the deathbed. So odd: even as you unconsciously arrange yourselves in the postures people have assumed for ages as they bid farewell to the ones they love, you cannot believe it is happening to you. My sister's face, red with tears. My distinguished brother, weeping at the foot of the bed. My husband on one side, me on the other. And Mom, her silver hair, that particular curve of her once-capable hand, the shape of her face and the plane of her cheekbone, never to be seen again. So still.

I wept, shaking my head up and down and back and forth, a combination of total recognition and inability to believe that she was really gone. "Thank you. Thank you. Thank you," I kept saying. It was a fusion of thanks to my mom, thanks to God for freeing her from the pain, thanks for what I could not see. I saw a dead body. I knew, with eye-stinging clarity, that she was alive. And I will see her again.

Like most artistic people, I have an endless capacity to envision doom. Even as a child I had identified the occasion of my mother's death as a dark-edged day of horror.

How like God to turn it inside out, to reverse my shadowed expectations! The day I had dreaded all my life became the doorway to real renewal. It was as if I tiptoed up to the dark gate, afraid of what I'd find, and it burst open with untrammeled freedom and joy. It wasn't the dog wearing Mom's nightgown. Thankfully. The doorway of death unleashed an absolute flood of gratitude that has rushed like a river over my life, reconfiguring my landscapes, overflowing my shallow places, nourishing a great thirst within me, and carrying me to new destinations far downstream where the vistas go on forever. Never have I felt so free, or eager: death makes it clear that each day of life is an opulent gift.

The good news is that these great realities and wild metaphors that I've been enjoying since my mom's death have not gone away. Though they are experiential in the fact that I've been experiencing them, they're not just feelings. They are rooted in fact, in the truths of the Gospel.

That means two things. First, their power can flow on days when my feelings ebb. And second, they can be shared in this book about gratitude and its gifts, that others might enjoy the great fountain of grace.

CHAPTER TWO

FOUNTAIN OF LIFE

We must be still and still moving
Into intensity
For a further union, a deeper communion
Through the dark cold and the empty desolation,
The wave cry, the wind cry, the vast waters
Of the petrel and the porpoise. In my end is my beginning.

T. S. Eliot, from "East Coker," *Four Quartets*

They feast on the abundance of your house;
    you give them drink from your river of delights.
For with you is the fountain of life;
    in your light we see light.

Psalm 36:8–9

In my mother's end was her beginning . . . and a new start for me as well. I had been spinning many plates for many months—work, home, children, church, kids' soccer, you name it. But my main focus had been on Mom. As we spun from crisis to crisis, I had built up tension inside as I yearned for her deliverance from pain and disease—even as I dreaded her departure. When that deliverance came, a dam broke. I felt a flood of God's grace, like a fountain, and as I thankfully lifted my face to feel its freshness, I realized I'd been dry for a while.

Friends told me I wasn't alone. Many said they felt dry too, like they were living in a spin cycle of spiritual fatigue. In the midst of life's demands—working hard, busily parenting, caring for friends and family in need, responding to daily challenges—it is easy to grow weary in well-doing. Conversely, when things are going smoothly, sometimes we slide away from God, lulled by the illusion we can do it all on our own. Either way, we can lose hold of the secret of staying connected to His power and keeping it current.

I thought of this when I helped prepare a party for several hundred adults at our children's school. The gym was a tropical paradise. There were balloons, palm trees, beach chairs. I wore my husband's Hawaiian shirt, a lei, and a cheery sun visor that gave me a terrible headache. This I tried to medicate by filching fudge every time I passed the dessert table.

My coworkers and I arranged platters of ripe pineapple and plump red strawberries, chilled silver plates of shrimp and lemon wedges. We stirred bubbling vats of hot crab dip and speared frilled toothpicks into sea scallops wrapped in fat ribbons of bacon. We set up a beverage table with an enormous fountain—the type of three-tiered apparatus one usually sees at a restaurant's Sunday brunch or a wedding reception. Not in the school gym.

Precariously balanced in the middle of a pink-skirted table, it was as tall as a fifth-grader. It had a wide, round bottom basin with silver spigots, a smaller middle level with spouts, and a top basin with a fountain and ivy-wrapped columns. In the center of this silver gazebo stood an elegant figurine, the Roman goddess of sparkling beverages. In our case, that would be lemonade.

A friend and I struggled with a heavy, thirty-gallon plastic tub of sloshing liquid refreshment. Yellow puddles slopped onto the gym floor. Spurred by adrenaline as we saw guests arriving, we dipped pitchers into it and doused the top tier of the fountain. The spigots and spouts flowed for a moment, then dribbled to a stop. We tried again. Dribbles, then drabs.

We reluctantly decided to read the directions, which were printed on a sticker on the underside of the bottom basin. I stuck my head under the cascading flowers that rimmed the silver brim. "To increase fountain flow," it said, "turn central figurine." I stuck my hand into the sticky lemonade and rotated the Roman lady. She wore a toga, had clusters of grapes in her hair, and looked indifferent. Turning her accomplished nothing. We poured in more and more pitchers, vainly hoping that doing the same thing, over and over, would somehow appease the lemonade goddess and the fountain would flow. Meanwhile thirsty people were circling the table, cups in hand.

Hauling the lemonade and our frenzied fiddling with the fountain had made us sweaty and frustrated. There was nothing else we could do.

Then someone had the radical thought: "Why don't we plug it in?"

Yes. Once connected to the power source, the fountain flowed, constantly replenished, and the thirsty guests began filling their cups.

The fountain at the school party is a picture that has often fit my life. Though I received Christ as a child, there have been many times over the years when I've tried to fill my fountain by my own luggy efforts—rather than being constantly refilled, and therefore able to nourish others, by the direct flow of His Holy Spirit.

Nothing new there. But in spite of how much I know that I must "remain in" Christ, as Jesus put it in John 15, my power cord slips so easily from the socket. And there I am again, sweating and toting that bale rather than bubbling with the Spirit's power. How, then, to remain plugged in?

This book is not about seven quick steps to spiritual power. But the secret of living in the passionate fountain of God's grace *is* accessible to all who are willing to practice a simple habit, every day. Every hour.

How do we stay connected to Christ?

What I have found is that the rhythm of divine renewal beats in the pulse of a purposefully grateful human heart. Our spiritual power depends on a moment-by-moment bond with God. And most simply, we build that bond by *thanking Him* in all things.

Now, *God* initiates and establishes our relationship with Him. We don't seek Him; He seeks us. He pursues us and saves us from sin and death. We were rebels in the enemy's camp; Christ rescues us and brings us Home. We have nothing to do with it. The Gospel truth is that there is no action we could have taken to be saved. Because of His great love for us, God makes us alive when we were dead. It's electrifying.

But once we're spiritually alive by God's power, we can act to remain plugged into His current of grace. Jesus said that we remain in Him by obeying Him, by keeping His commandments.[1] One of the simplest ways to do so, one that's often neglected because it's so basic, is to engage in the perpetual dialogue of gratitude.

This is not just an option for believers who want to splash in waves of grace, and those who prefer to be miserable are exempt. God *commands* His followers to be thankful. (Some spend a lot of time wondering about God's will for their lives. We can be absolutely certain of at least one aspect of His divine will: we are to be thankful! We are to give thanks! In all things!)

The apostle Paul wrote to believers in Thessalonica,

> Be joyful always; pray continually; give thanks in all circumstances, for this is God's will for you in Christ Jesus.[2]

And to the Colossians:

> Let the peace of Christ rule in your hearts, since as members of one body you were called to peace. And be thankful. Let the word of Christ dwell in you richly as you teach and admonish one another with all wisdom, and as you sing psalms, hymns and spiritual songs with gratitude in your hearts to God. And whatever you do, whether in word or deed, do it all in the name of the Lord Jesus, giving thanks to God the Father through him.[3]

And to the Philippians:

> Rejoice in the Lord always. I will say it again: Rejoice! Let your gentleness be evident to all. The Lord is near. Do not be anxious about anything, but in everything, by prayer and petition, with thanksgiving, present your requests to God. And the peace of God, which transcends all understanding, will guard your hearts and your minds in Christ Jesus.[4]

It's incredible: The small, compliant human action of saying "thank you" constantly links us to the awesome Creator of the universe. In the practice of perceiving every part of every day as a gift from Him, we stay connected to Christ. We can't wander away, as our hearts are so prone to do: as we thank God for His presents, we remain in His presence. He says, "You are welcome." And more. We begin to see things from His point of view. The conversations of a continually grateful heart become a way of life, a fountain flowing in us, the means by which we acknowledge our dependence on Christ, enjoy Him lavishly, and run to do whatever He wants.

In this perspective, it's important to realize there are two types of gratitude. They often mingle together in the life of a follower of Christ. But we must take a moment to stop and discern them clearly, for one is secondary, the other primary.

The secondary sort is thankfulness for blessings received. Life, health, home, family, freedom, a warm bed, a tall, cool drink on a warm June day—it's a mindset of active appreciation for all good gifts, large, small, spiritual, emotional, material.

In his classic *Religious Affections*, Jonathan Edwards called thanks for such blessings "natural gratitude." This is a good thing. But it is not, on its own, sufficient to stir us to true love for the Giver. Edwards says that if people love God *only* because of what He gives them, their affection begins at the wrong end. (Perhaps he was thinking of the tail wagging the dog, for he goes on to say that "even a dog will love his master that is kind to him.")[5] Or, to paraphrase Jesus, even pagans can give thanks when things are going well. But such gratitude does not come naturally when things go badly. It cannot buoy us in difficult times. Nor, *by itself*, does it truly please God.

Edwards called the fundamental, primary form of thankfulness "gracious gratitude." It gives thanks for *who God is*. It gives thanks for His character—His goodness, love, power, excellencies—regardless of any favors received. It is the real evidence of the Holy Spirit in a person's life. Gracious gratitude can grow in the midst of pain, trouble, and distress. We hear it in the intimate whispers of the psalmist who longs to know God more deeply even as enemies surround him. We see it in the otherwise inexplicable surety of Job: "Though You slay me, yet will I trust in You." We feel it in the apostle Paul's contentment regardless of his circumstances. If threatened with death, he says: "Fine. To die is gain!" If kept alive, fine again: "For me to live is Christ!" He was unstoppable, unquenchable, full of thanks and peace and joy, not because of what he had, but Who he knew.

This gracious gratitude for *who God is* also goes to the heart of *who we are* in Christ. It is relational, rather than conditional. Though our world may shatter, we are secure in Him. Like Paul, we can have peace in uncertainty or pain. The fount of our joy, the love of the God who made us and saved us, cannot be quenched by any power that exists.[6]

Those who are full of gracious gratitude overflow like a fountain. They're brimming with joy, worship, and mission. They bear witness to the One who saved them, both by how they live and what they say. They're irrepressible. They go wherever God leads, wherever there are needs. They can't be stopped by opposition, convention, or any other obstacle.

This kind of gratitude grows throughout the lifetime of the believer, irrespective of circumstances. As we become more and more aware—through the Scriptures' truth and the Spirit's power—of how desperately sinful we really are, we also become more and more astounded by how righteous God really is. We see more and more clearly that God is God, wholly and holy Other, not some manageable deity we've made up in our own small minds. We recognize the impossible gap between our sinfulness and His holiness. It is insurmountable—but for the cross, which bridges that chasm. We look to the cross and are overwhelmed by the love of Christ, His blood poured out to make us right with God.

Though Jonathan Edwards probably didn't have to manage a lemonade fountain at his children's school, his writings are full of this bubbling image. "Love is the fountain of all the affections," he wrote. From it springs "a sweet and melting gratitude to God, for His great goodness."[7]

Hot gratitude melts our hard pride. Again, it is the means of remaining in Christ. This thanksgiving for who He is mingles with daily thanks for all good gifts, from breath in our lungs to asparagus in the springtime. Relishing who God is and all He's given is the secret of remaining connected to Him—and also of sucking the marrow from every ordinary day.

This book is of course not the exhaustive tome on such an enormous topic. All I know is that I would be remiss if I did not tell the stories I've been given, woven with Scripture, of how God can refresh real people through the gracious gift of radical gratitude.

And it's no surprise, really, that it was one of life's sad endings that began a new experience of gratitude in my own life. Times of brokenness tend to bind us to God more closely than seasons when we are comfortable and self-sufficient. Death spotlights what is truly important. Loss clarifies priorities. Both amplify God's still, small truths that are sometimes drowned out in the clatter of everyday life.

That was certainly my experience just after my mother's death.

CHAPTER THREE

WHISPERS IN THE NIGHT

Christ be with me, Christ within me,
Christ behind me, Christ before me,
Christ beside me, Christ to win me;
Christ to comfort and restore me;
Christ beneath me, Christ above me,
Christ in quiet, Christ in danger,
Christ in hearts of all that love me,
Christ in mouth of friend and stranger.

From "St. Patrick's Breastplate," fifth century

Since we had to wait our turn in Arlington National Cemetery's long queue of military burials, several weeks passed between Mom's death and funeral. We made arrangements, arranged for trumpeters to play the hymns she loved, and wrote a death notice for the *Washington Post*. One sunny afternoon I drove to the mortuary to meet with Bill, our funeral-home person. He gave me a brown envelope and a small oak box. Inside the box was a plastic bag secured with a yellow twist-tie, a few pounds of ashes that had been my mom. These "cremains," as Bill called them, were what would be interred. Inside the envelope was something we had forgotten to slip from Mom's wrist the day she died. Her watch. So odd that it was still keeping time, and she was not.

I placed the little oak box on the hearth next to a big vase full of gladiolas. Bill also gave me my own small bag of ashes as a keepsake. It seemed fitting to tuck this into a bright blue-and-white soup tureen on the sideboard. Meanwhile the children and I talked about where Grannis really was now, and just what was in those plastic bags.

Such discussions in our home were superseded by events in our community. An unknown sniper was targeting people around Washington, killing men and women as they pumped gas, mowed lawns, loaded grocery bags in their cars. A woman was slain outside a post office; a teenager was shot at his school. The dead included an engineer who had earned a Purple Heart in Vietnam. A nanny. A bus driver. A cancer survivor.

As each new shooting was breathlessly announced on breaking news bulletins, the tension rose. It was all too easy to envision yourself in the sniper's crosshairs. People crouched beside their cars as they pumped gas and ran in zigzags after they parked their cars. Police officers patrolled the schools. A tall plywood barrier was erected outside our daughter's fifth-grade classroom to obstruct what would otherwise be a clear line of fire from the woods. Recess, soccer, and football games were canceled. Dragnets stalled traffic for hours as police searched in vain for a white van that just might belong to the sniper.

In the end, ten people were killed and three were wounded. Police arrested a seventeen-year-old and his "mentor." The shootings stopped. The plywood barriers came down. We walked in straight lines again.

My mother's death had been sad, but it was also the outcome she had desired. She had lived a long, full life. She was in pain, confident in Christ, ready to be delivered.

But these sniper shootings were another story. They reeked of the dark designs of the Enemy . . . allowed by God, surely, but quite difficult to accept and impossible to explain. They were horrifyingly random and somehow even more terrifying to many than the terrorist attack on the Pentagon a year earlier. The victims were black, white, young, old, shopping at Home Depot, doing the mundane tasks that weave each day's tapestry of ordinary life, ruptured when the shooter peered through the sights of his Bushmaster XM–15 rifle, settled on someone, and squeezed the trigger. "Call me God," he wrote in a taunting note to police.

"It has been a challenge," said the brother of one of the victims. "But a long time ago, we chose to trust God rather than question Him. There were two inches between my brother being hit and not being hit. Who am I to question something like this?"[1]

I woke often in the night, startled by dreams. I'd sit up in bed, my heart pounding. Had someone fallen? I must be needed somewhere. Then I'd remember that I didn't have to try to rescue Mom any more. She wasn't in a broken heap, moaning and needing help. She was safe where pain could not touch her.

I'd creep out of bed and check on the children. Walker would be on his bottom bunk, flung like a starfish that had washed up on shore, his spine bent back in an improbably reversed C. In her room, his twin Haley would be tucked in her top bunk, hand under her cheek and her body bent in a graceful forward arc that neatly complemented her brother's backward one. Meanwhile Emily would be propped on an extra pillow, her mouth moving as she continued the day's conversations in the dialogues of her dreams.

All safe. No one to rescue. No sniper. No terrorists.

It would take a while to go back to sleep. And in the night I could hear, over and over, an echoing, certain heartbeat. *I love you. I love you. I love you*, God seemed to whisper.

Why did I feel His comfort? Because all was calm, all was bright? Because there was no crisis in the Vaughn home?

Yes, but no. This respiration of grace exceeded each day's events. I could breathe in the words of the Scriptures that are whispered to us all in the watches of the night, any night, in times of peace and prosperity, poverty and pain. *I am here*, says the Lord. *Fear not. I am with you always. Fear not. I have called you by name. You are Mine. And even the darkness is as light to Me.*

For me, that October's strange days and long nights led to a new experience of gratitude through a morbid means. They reminded me that death is coming. It creeps gradually to some, as in Mom's slow decline. For others, it is the sudden explosion on a golden fall afternoon. Two inches to the right, and life would have gone on.

Sometimes, in crisis, the reality of death is unavoidable. More often, though, it is comfortably distant. It happens to people far away, people we don't know. Or it is real, of course, but won't intrude until the distant future, when we are old and somehow ready. It's easy to deny its approach.

But the fact that death is coming, one way or another, can be a useful tool, the Swiss Army knife of everyday life. It can serve a variety of good purposes, if we let it.

For one, it cuts through the clutter and clarifies priorities. Death helps us live with one eye on eternity, the other on the ordinary day in front of us, and rather than making us cross-eyed, to stay with the metaphor, it helps us focus on the Cross. Thanks to Christ's staggering sacrifice, we will live forever. In thanks to Him, we choose to invest our time and energies in what matters most.

The starkest picture of this clarity of priority came in the cellphone calls made on the morning of September 11, 2001. Aboard their doomed planes, and from the highest floors of New York's flaming towers, did people fondly peruse their stock portfolios one last time? Did they review their to-do lists? Did they call their brokers, bosses, agents, or decorators? No. They called the people they loved.

A woman named Rosa received one of those calls.

Six months after the terrorist attacks, I visited with Rosa. She is a slim woman with capable, expressive hands, dark hair, erect posture, clear eyes. She tells her story in a flood of Spanish as our friend Lois translates. Her husband, Junior, had worked at Windows on the World, on the 106th floor of World Trade Center Tower One. His story takes shape as she speaks; it's as if she is drawing their lives on big sheets of art paper. She uses quick, sure strokes. I can see his smiling face, feel her relief that he has finally received Christ and quit drinking. I hear him teasing her and playing games with the children. Rosa has a CD with her, and we listen to the solo he sang in church. I see them going, as a family, on the church retreat. They sleep in cabins, eat in the dining hall, go on a scavenger hunt. She feels like it is a new beginning, a happy dream. They are a real family; she has never seen Junior so full of joy. They return to the city during the first week of September. Though Junior is still on vacation, he volunteers to work for someone else on September 10 and 11. On the morning of the 11th, he leaves home at 6:20. He kisses her good-bye.

She happens to be on the phone with him when the first plane hits. He tells her he'll call her right back after he finds out what happened. He doesn't know. Neither does she. But by the time he calls a few minutes later, she has turned on the television and seen the inferno beneath him. "It's filling with smoke," he tells her. "We've got wet towels. We're going to try to get out—"

The line goes dead.

"I started crying out to the Lord," Rosa tells me, weeping even as her voice is strong, a rippling current flowing like a stream. "Oh, God! Oh, God! Be with him! Take care of him!"

As she prays her mind is full of the story of Shadrach, Meshach, and Abednego. God had rescued them from the fire. God could rescue Junior.

King Nebuchadnezzar was one of the great conquerors of ancient history. He was also given to fits of rage and insanity. At this point in his story, he decreed that anyone who did not worship according to his mandate would be executed.

The three Hebrew exiles refused to do so. "O Nebuchadnezzar . . . ," they said, "if we are thrown into the blazing furnace, the God we serve is able to save us from it, and He will rescue us from your hand, O king. But even if He does not, we want you to know, O king, that we will not serve your gods."[2]

Furious, the king ordered his men to prepare the furnace. It was a large brick kiln equipped with vents and bellows, a big hole at the top, and a smaller opening at the bottom, through which the men could be viewed. Nebuchadnezzar commanded his soldiers to tie up the three young men and throw them into the flames. The heat killed the soldiers even as they hoisted Shadrach, Meshach, and Abednego into the air. Tightly tied, the three tumbled into the deep furnace.

From a safe distance, Nebuchadnezzar peered into the inferno and leapt to his feet.

"Weren't there three men that we tied up and threw into the fire?" he shouted at his advisers.

They knew to always agree with the king, and besides, it was true. "Certainly, O king," they cried.

"Look!" the king shrieked. "I see four men walking around in the fire, unbound and unharmed, and the fourth looks like a son of the gods."

He called for Shadrach, Meshach, and Abednego. They came out of the fire. And they didn't even smell like smoke.

Four days after New York's inferno, Rosa knows that Junior is gone. She perseveres, one day at a time. She takes care of her children; her church takes care of her.

Meanwhile, in the smoking ruins of the towers, workers search desperately for all that was lost. A wind ruffles the ash. Shreds of papers that were once important swirl in a whirlwind over the pile. A searcher finds a tibia. A femur. Improbably, another finds a laminated card: there is a mustache and a smiling face. It is Junior's driver's license. And that is all that remains.

So Junior was not miraculously rescued from the fire like the men who walked free from Nebuchadnezzar's furnace. Rosa thinks about "the fourth man, the one who looks like a son of the gods." Was he an angel? Christ Himself? It is a mystery. But she knows one thing: When Junior's own fire came, he was not alone. *Emmanuel.* God was with him.

In our lives, too, *death reminds us that God is with us.* Always. The imminence of death can point us to the immanence of God.

God was with all who died on September 11, as a poem passed around the Internet puts it. I'm reluctant to quote from an email that was forwarded to just about everyone in America—but it was circulated so widely precisely because it touched a common chord. It's not a sophisticated piece of writing. But it pulls at something elemental that mourns and aches and longs inside all of us. It is as if God is speaking, and reads, in part:

> . . . I was on all four of those planes, in every seat, with every prayer. I was with the crew as they were overtaken. I was in the very hearts of the believers there, comforting and assuring them that their faith has saved them.
>
> I was in Texas, Kansas, London. I was standing next to you when you heard the terrible news. Did you sense Me?
>
> I want you to know that I saw every face. I knew every name—though not all know Me. Some met Me for the first time on the 86th floor.
>
> Some sought Me with their last breath. Some couldn't hear Me calling to them through the smoke and flames; "Come to Me . . . this way . . . take My hand." Some chose, for the final time, to ignore Me. But I was there."[3]

God is with us.

Death can also remind us that each day is a gift.

Those who died in the flames of September 11—and the loved ones they left behind—would give a different perspective than the mindset we carry on the "business as usual" days of our lives. If they could watch us scurrying along, hearts cold, minds preoccupied, bodies stressed, they would shout at us all: Fall on your knees! Breathe it in! Thank God! Each day is a gift!

The familiar play that points to this perspective is Thornton Wilder's *Our Town.* Written long before the alien terrors of the twenty-first century, it spotlights the ordinary moments of daily life and relationships. It is heartbreaking.

Emily, a young woman who dies in childbirth in the early 1900s, is allowed the opportunity to revisit one day of her life on earth. She chooses her twelfth birthday, fourteen years earlier. There is a hot breakfast on a snowy morning, a bright blue ribbon for her hair, her mother's hug, her father's voice calling, "Where's my birthday girl?"

It all slips away. "Good-bye!" calls Emily. "Good-bye! Good-bye to clocks ticking . . . and Mama's sunflowers. And food and coffee. And new-ironed dresses and hot baths . . . and sleeping and waking up. Oh, earth, you're too wonderful for anybody to realize you."

She breaks into tears. "Do human beings ever realize life while they live it?—every, every minute?"

"No," comes the answer from the plain-spoken narrator. "The saints and poets, maybe—they do some."[4]

God's grace makes the worst of us saints even as it frees us all to perceive like poets. We are peculiar people of two worlds, and the one illumines the other. On one hand we look to the dazzling luxuries of unfathomable eternity with Christ. On the other, Christ's presence with us and His good purposes for us give rich meaning to the ordinary glories of our days here. Every one is a gift.

Similarly, *death can remind believers that we don't have to really die*—and so compel us right into an overwhelming mindset of gratitude.

Most of us don't receive stunning visions that confirm that fact. We see only death's aftermath, the shell of the person we loved.

When I held my mom's dead hand, there was nothing left of Mildred there. She was gone. "Absent from the body, present with the Lord," is what the Scriptures say. I certainly couldn't see the "present with the Lord" part. But I knew it was true.

A friend lost his father to cancer a few years ago. Mr. Walker was in the hospital for some time, and then the family decided to bring him home for his last days. They set up his bed in the living room overlooking the Chesapeake Bay.

Mr. Walker's huge chocolate Labrador, Ambrose, was so excited that his master had returned that he would jump up on his bed, nuzzling, squishing, and licking him. Kicked off by family members, he stayed under the bed, never more than a few feet away from his master.

During his dad's final hours, my friend Paul left the dog downstairs. After Mr. Walker passed on, however, he let the dog back in, thinking Ambrose might make a final farewell in his own way.

The dog ran into the room, sniffing this way and that, looking frantically. Mr. Walker was still on the bed, in the same position in which he had lain for days. The dog circled the room, nosed the bed, then ran onward, still searching. He knew what we all know: his master's body might have been on that bed, but the real Mr. Walker, the man he had loved, was gone.

We can't find our loved ones either. We cherish the lingering scent in their clothes, the strands of hair clinging in a brush, the ashes in the little bag. My best friend Patti, who lost her athletic, hilarious husband to cancer in 1992, recently found a Xerox copy he had made of a small document. He had pressed the paper flat on the copier's glass surface ... and so there was John's large hand, the whorls of his fingers, the curve of his lifeline, gone yet preserved, a smudged link to all that was lost, the husband she had and could no longer hold.

Such a mystery.

Years ago I visited South Carolina in order to write about a man named Rusty.[5] His story was surreal in some ways, for Rusty was privy to information known only to God in most of our cases: the exact hour of his own death.

Rusty had committed horrible crimes. Then, on death row, he received Christ. Rusty repented, asked forgiveness of his victims' families, mourned over his drug use that had so corrupted him. He was ready, he said, for the state's ultimate punishment.

One April midnight, officers shaved Rusty's head, shackled his arms and legs, and walked him to the execution chamber. The official witnesses sat in two short rows facing the electric chair. The warden stood next to a wall that held three telephones: open lines to the deputy commissioner, the attorney general, the governor.

Officers secured Rusty in the big wooden chair, buckling heavy leather restraining straps over his chest, legs, and arms.

"Do you have a final statement?" the warden asked.

"I'm sorry," Rusty said. "I claim Jesus Christ as my Savior. My only wish is that everyone in the world could feel the love I have felt from Him."

The electrician fitted Rusty's head into a leather beanie connected to a thick electrode descending from the ceiling. He strapped another electrode to Rusty's leg, fastened the copper headpiece over his head, and dropped the leather death hood over his face.

Darkness.

Rusty could hear the warden's voice making the final phone check to see if the governor had intervened. It sounded far away. He could hear an officer escorting someone out. He could sense the executioners nervously waiting for the warden's order to hit the triggers that would activate the killing current.

The seconds ticked by. Darkness under the hood.

Then the jolt of two thousand volts.

Light.

The dark reality of death reminds us that we are all but a heartbeat away from eternal light. It pierces the blinders of the everyday comforts, complacency, and misery in this world. For the believer, when death comes, it brings us home.

Earlier generations knew this well. They walked lightly in this world, for they knew they were just a-passin' through. So do believers in the persecuted church today and in suffering or needy places. To them, heaven is not just a vague pleasantry that sounds quaint and slightly dull, but a blinding, golden hope that diminishes earthly pain by the sheer enormity of its weight of glory.

Yet so many of us in North America are quite comfortable right here, thank you. Not sure we're ready to go. (As one younger friend put it, "At least let me get married first!") And popular culture seems to be in a massive case of denial about death, which is understandable if indeed this life is all there is. It's far more soothing to hawk an improbable posture of perpetual youth. Almost eighty, Hugh Hefner pops Viagra like Pez and has seven girlfriends. Any sagging body part can be nipped, tucked, injected, or augmented. And in the end you can indulge in the ultimate plastic surgery and have a brain-lift, your head cryonically frozen so you can come back to life (or, as cheerful marketing materials put it, be "reanimated") later—just as long as your estate keeps paying the freezer company.

What a pitiful thought! Those who believe the Gospel would pay *not* to come back. Death holds no ultimate terrors. Sadness, yes, and mourning; sometimes horror, violence, and awful pain. Yes, it is hideous.

But in the end, death is engulfed, swallowed up in Christ's absolute victory over the worst that Satan could do. On this side of the dark river, we cannot imagine the laughter on the other side—feasting, joy, thundering, rainbowed waterfalls of freedom.

The reality of death can be a useful tool. It can remind us of the eternal perspective that prioritizes daily life, the great fact of God's presence with us and His provision for us. And in the shaky uncertainties of this world, it boots us right toward heaven, the everlasting rule of the God who irresistibly loves us.

"Therefore, since we are receiving a kingdom that cannot be shaken, let us be thankful, and so worship God acceptably with reverence and awe, for our 'God is a consuming fire.' "[6]

Let us be thankful.

CHAPTER FOUR

BE THE ONE!

Now on his way to Jerusalem, Jesus traveled along the border between
Samaria and Galilee. As he was going into a village, ten men who had
leprosy met him. They stood at a distance and called out in a loud voice,
"Jesus, Master, have pity on us!"

When he saw them, he said, "Go, show yourselves to the priests."
And as they went, they were cleansed.

One of them, when he saw he was healed, came back, praising God
in a loud voice. He threw himself at Jesus' feet and thanked him—
and he was a Samaritan.

Jesus asked, "Were not all ten cleansed? Where are the other nine?"

Luke 17:11–17

When I was younger, lepers were shadowy Bible figures who
didn't seem quite real. After all, I'd never met anyone with
leprosy.

But then I went to a remote village in India that was not part of
the modern world. Far from civilization, it was inaccessible by car.
We left our jeep at the bottom of a rocky, dusty hill and found the
entrance to a narrow path upwards. Huge boulders marked the
spot; three had been painted with the sign of the cross.

At the top of the rocky hill was a small, stone church with banners and flags fluttering in the breeze. Nearby was a cluster of small

wooden shacks about the size of garden sheds. It was near Christmas; a big star hung in the branches of a knobby tree near one of the huts.

As we clambered up the path, people from the little community spotted us and began to gather. There were children, a few healthy men and women ... and a number who were afflicted with leprosy. They held strips of dusty fabric to cover the lower part of their faces; their heads and feet were bound as well. But a few wore sandals, and I could see their toeless feet. Some had no fingers. Some were missing parts of their noses and ears.

They came toward us as fast as they could, the stronger helping the weaker. We gathered in a big circle, and they led us in singing praises to God.

Since that impromptu worship service, I've been able to better visualize all those lepers in the Bible.

In Jesus' day, leprosy and other skin diseases were cause for terrible fear and shame. Lepers were ostracized and could return to their community only if a priest had declared them fit. Old Testament law held that a person "with such an infectious disease must wear torn clothes, let his hair be unkempt, cover the lower part of his face and cry out, 'Unclean! Unclean!' As long as he has the infection he remains unclean. He must live alone; he must live outside the camp."[1]

Unclean! Unclean!

One day about two thousand years ago, Jesus was on the outskirts of a village not too different from the rural towns I saw in India. As He's on the road, ten tattered lepers call to Him from afar. They dare not draw nearer.

"Jesus, Master, have pity on us!"

Jesus' heart moves for them. He tells them to go show themselves to the local priest.

Off they go. Faltering but hopeful.

And as they are going, the Scriptures say, they are healed.

The ten stumble along the road, ragged robes flapping. Bystanders scurry away as they see the lepers coming.

As the men hurry, the dirty rags fall from their faces. I can imagine what happened next.

"Hiram!" shouts one. "Your nose!"

"What do mean, my nose?" says Hiram, bustling along.

"You've got one!"

"Aaugghghh!"

Piling to a stop, slamming into one another like clowns at the circus, they stare at each other's faces, mouths wide open. They unwind the rags from their hands, shouting because they have fingers again. They leap into the air; they land, sure-footed. They strip off their bonds and clap their arms around each other's shoulders, laughing with joy. They can't wait to find their families. They sprint toward town.

But one whirls and turns in the other direction, back toward Jesus. He runs fast with his new feet. Weeping, he falls and kisses Jesus' perfect ones.

"Thank You!" he sobs. *Thank You. Thank You.*

Ten were rescued, cleansed, given a brand-new beginning. Yet nine ran the wrong way. Only one ran for Home base, where Jesus was.

Friends of ours have a family mantra. "Be the one!" they tell their kids and each other. "Be the one who thanks Jesus. Let others go where they may. You be the one who is grateful."

Be the one!

Being thankful is not rocket science. Though the topic of gratitude goes as deep as the grace of God, it does not require tough biblical exegesis or advanced degrees to practice it. It just requires obedience.

Some believers seem to be looking for life principles that are just a little more spiritually sexy. Be thankful? Oh, of course. But give me something more exciting, more dramatic, something remarkable that I can do to change my life.

As one friend told me, "I don't think gratitude is the right topic for a book. People today want quick answers. They don't want gradual process. They want a proven formula that will change their lives."

We live in an instant culture. Minute Rice? Who has the time? That mindset has leaked into our theology. Who wouldn't want to experience instant change, the spiritual version of television's makeover shows? Something like *Trading Spaces*: forty-eight hours to a fresh, new look. Or an extreme makeover: submit yourself to an assault of reconstructive surgeries, and once you recover you won't even recognize yourself. You'll have to wear a name tag on your brand-new chest. Or maybe the sanctification story *My Heart, Christ's Home* meets one of those design programs where the homeowner goes away from the weekend: we come home, and find that the Holy Spirit has been busily cleaning and redecorating our spiritual lives, and we didn't have to do a thing.

Few of us want to cozy up to the fact that most often God changes us in the process of ordinary day-to-day dependence on Him. We change most not in the great dramas of life, but in the small acts of submission that no one sees but Him, like when we thank Him in a hard circumstance, rather than railing, "Why me?" (As Ravi Zacharias has noted, people never wail, "Why me?" when they win the lottery.)

Developing the meditative habit of constantly whispering thanks to Him—no matter the situation—is in fact a mustard seed of life-changing power. Radical, for it goes to the root of who we are. Small, seemingly insignificant, yet it has the power to change our lives and blow our socks off, right in the midst of the every-day. When we really give God thanks in everything, we are acknowledging that He is sovereign and that we trust Him. And we find that it changes us.

For example, a friend was going through the wringer with her teenage daughter. Their once-close relationship had devolved into a briar patch of prickly feelings, stinging barbs, and angry outbursts. My friend felt she could not utter a sentence without stepping into a minefield. Her patience was waning, her frustration growing. The conflicts with her daughter were affecting other relationships, like with her husband.

My friend decided to hold on—like a dog with a savory bone—to God's presence with her in these challenges. Every time she saw her daughter or got into a difficult conversation, she would clench her teeth around God's truth. Thank You that You are with me! Thank You for giving me this girl! Thank You that she is even able to speak! Thank You that her mind works so quickly! Thank You that the story is not yet over! Thank You for Your patience with *me*!

She thanked God when she didn't feel thankful, right in the midst of the fray, every day. Several things happened.

First, this exercise titillated a creative challenge within her as she sought to discern all the things she could thank God for. Second, it distanced her from the emotion of the moment, so she didn't respond to her daughter out of frustration or anger. She found she was thinking more about God than her daughter. Third, that distance allowed her to actually see humor in various situations. Humor is good. And fourth, the more she thanked God for her daughter, the more she was able to perceive her as *His* daughter. She found that developing the habit of giving thanks gave her more resilience and elasticity, rather than always being ready to snap. And oddly enough, she couldn't wait for her daughter to get home from school every day, so she could lavish love on her. My friend's act of obedience to God—thanking Him in all things—actually changed not only her mind, but her emotions.

This kind of habitual gratitude is not unique to Christianity. Buddhism, Hinduism, and Islam commend thankfulness as a morally beneficial state that produces reciprocal kindnesses. The Koran also teaches that true gratitude draws more blessings upon the believer, as in Allah's promise, "If you are grateful, I will give you more."[2]

In classical Western tradition, the Roman sage Cicero called gratitude not only the greatest of virtues but the parent of all others. Though Aristotle saw it as a weakness that "soon grows old," Plato and Socrates wrote that citizens have a duty of obedience to the state based on gratitude for its benefits. Shakespeare wrote, "O Lord that lends me life, lend me a heart replete with thankfulness!" Immanuel Kant said that ingratitude was the "essence of vileness." In America, our national heritage has been powerfully shaped by the "covenant" we keep with those who have gone before, that national service and public duty are in fact a debt of gratitude we owe our forefathers and foremothers, who sacrificed their blood, tears, sweat, and toil to secure the liberties we enjoy.

Perhaps it is no surprise that many of today's spins on the topic are more individualistic in nature, focusing less on gratitude's part in our national fabric and more on its personal benefits. A few minutes ago I searched the Internet and found 1,280,000 hits that would lead me to sites about thankfulness.

Some will remind you that a habit of thankfulness has proven health benefits. For example, several university psychologists recently conducted a Research Project on Gratitude and Thanksgiving. They divided participants into three groups. People in the first group practiced daily gratitude exercises, like keeping a list of things for which they were grateful. They reported higher levels of alertness, enthusiasm, determination, optimism, and energy. They also experienced less depression and stress than the control group. (Unsurprisingly, they were also a *lot* happier than the group of study participants who were directed to keep a daily journal of all the *bad* things that happened to them each day.)

One of the psychologists concluded that though a practice of gratitude is a substantial part of most religions, its benefits extend to the general population, regardless of faith or lack thereof. He suggested that anyone can increase his sense of well-being and create positive social effects just from counting his blessings.[3] (True enough—as far as Edwards's "natural gratitude" can take you.)

Also on the Internet's consumer playground, you can shop for gratitude products like diaries, posters, or thank you cards. Or you can journal the five things you're grateful for each day, interacting, if you want, with thousands of unknown web friends, an online fellowship of gratitude. You can light a virtual candle in cyberspace—shielding it so it won't be blown out by a virtual breeze—or practice gratitude with "self-empowerment," or be reminded to thank the people who bless your life. Or you can buy a calendar cautioning that perhaps you spend too much time expressing gratitude to others, so you just must make sure to "first of all, thank yourself."

Then, while I was still busy thanking myself, I found another website, this one promoting a book about "the life-giving practice of gratitude."

> Close your eyes. Sit up straight. Take [a] deep breath. As you exhale think . . . thank you.
> Do it again, please.
> Thank you.
> Who were you thanking? God? The Universe? Yourself? No one in particular? It doesn't really matter. It feels good no matter who you're thanking—especially when it's for nothing, or everything.[4]

Though the object of gratitude—to *whom* we are grateful—is up for grabs, it's hard to find anyone who would argue that gratitude is not a great thing.

Last winter I went away for a writing week to a friend's home in a New Jersey beach town. Late one afternoon I was sitting on a bench on the boardwalk, drinking coffee and staring at the ocean. A man wearing a red leather jacket appeared. He settled on the next bench and started talking. He worked construction, he said. His wife had left him for a state trooper. He liked to come and sit by the ocean after work. He advised me where to get the best cannoli in town. He told me about his kids, his health, his job, his mother. He was ever so slightly lonely.

"So what do you do?" he asked.

I told him, "Not much," that mostly I just sat around and drank coffee, though I was writing a book about gratitude in my spare time.

"Gratitude? That's great," he said, rapping his knuckles on his head. "Yeah, knock on wood, I got my health, and I always thank the Man Upstairs for that!"

This is a potentially lovely thought, with its intuitive sense that all good gifts come from above—though I would take issue with the theology of the Man Upstairs.

If "to whom it may concern" gratitude is a modern-day virtue, how much more so is it for those who've been actually rescued from death and hell by Jesus Christ? Should not we, like the thankful ex-leper, be leaping and running to thank Him, every single day of our lives?

Truly grateful people can't be stopped. They bubble and overflow, refreshing others. Their habitual gratitude serves as a springboard to give a reason for the buoyant hope bouncing within them. They attract those who are stuck in the cares of this world, and woo them to the eternal Good.

Years ago there was an incident on the Washington subway system in which a crowded train stalled on an underground track. Harried commuters were beside themselves. No one had been talking to one another, but now they burst into mutual, frenzied spurts of accusations against the driver—as if the situation was under his control—the Metro authorities, the federal government, anyone and everyone they could blame for this vile inconvenience.

Somewhere in the midst of all this invective, a woman with a number of bulky shopping bags dropped a new bottle of perfume, and it shattered. Within a few minutes, the pure, luxurious fragrance had wafted the length of the crowded car.

It was as if the fresh smell released people from a dark spell. They sniffed, smiled, and relaxed, laughing with each other. Surprise!

Followers of Jesus have the opportunity, in life's crowded moments when people feel stuck, to *be* the fragrance of Christ. We don't need to be annoying Pollyannas (who would be thrown right off the Metro anyway), but free spirits—saints and poets—who can lead, turn the tide, rather than follow along on the lazy downward spiral of negativity. What it takes is a purposeful, daily decision on our part to *be the one.* Then follows the creative question in the bad situation, a smile, compassion, a little humor that suggests that we need not take our small selves so seriously . . . a look upward and outward, where the vistas of God's great love call us to come and enjoy Him, now and forever.

Sometimes a particular event serves as the catalyst for the overflow of gratitude. For example, Colonel Brian Birdwell was just yards away from the impact point of the fifty-ton 757 jetliner that crashed into the Pentagon on September 11, 2001.

One moment he was walking back to his office after a trip to the restroom. In the next there was a deafening explosion. Wind, choking smoke and dust, ceiling tiles, steel girders, wall panels, flying glass—it must have been a bomb. Brian found himself on his back. Above and ahead, he could see only billowing blackness. But in his immediate visual field there was an orange glow, a corona around him that lit the darkness. At first he didn't know where it was coming from. Then he realized it was him. He was on fire, a human torch.

The pain was indescribable. But the physical sensation was less than his emotional shock. *I am dying*, his brain registered. *This is the end. I am thirty-nine years old, I left my office to go to the men's room, and now I am burning to death. I'll never see my wife and son again.* It was like standing on familiar ground, at ease one moment— and then, without warning, plummeting from a lofty cliff.

Brian had been trained to fight. He tried to get up, but his legs wouldn't work. He couldn't even roll. His life's thin cord had snapped, and now it was unspooling, out of control, burning right through his hands down to this very moment. This was his death, and as he hurtled toward it, he found his faith was real. It was a knot at life's end that he could hold on to.

"Jesus, I'm coming to see You!" Brian shouted.

Then he waited. Waited for whatever it feels like when the soul departs the human body. He did not feel afraid, though he did feel small, dwarfed: one slight, modest life about to enter the immeasurable enormity of eternity.

He lay in the darkness, burning, in agony, yet at peace. Waiting. Waiting.

The next thing he knew, there was a stream running down his cheek. Not blood, nor tears, but a shower of cool water from the Pentagon sprinkler system. Brian had fallen right beneath a sprinkler nozzle. The spray of water doused his burning body, and gradually put him out.

Brian told me that he doesn't remember much about the months that followed. Unconsciousness. Horrific pain. Surgeries upon surgeries. Excruciating rehabilitation. But in the midst of it all, he was stunned—and thankful—to be alive. His gratitude overflowed into outreach to others: Brian and his wife, Mel, started a ministry to people who had suffered similar injuries. They began visiting burn centers across the U.S., giving patients and their families help in the midst of pain so terrible that only those who have experienced it can really offer hope.[5]

Few of us experience events quite as dramatic as Brian's. But for all of us, as with his case, gratitude for God's deliverance reveals itself in *action*.

My husband and some friends were in Cuba a few weeks ago. Along with local believers, they visited homes in small villages. They were welcomed in by curious Cubans. Over and over, Lee and his team told the "bad news, good news" story of Jesus. (The bad news is that we have all sinned. . . . The good news is that Jesus paid the penalty for sin.)

The Holy Spirit moved in hundreds of Cubans' lives. In one rural village, a young man who had just given his life to Christ ran out into the unpaved road in front of his house, waving his arms and yelling to his neighbors. *¡Venido aquí!* "Come here!" he shouted. *¡Tengo buenas noticias!* "I've got good news!" *¡Usted tiene que oír esto!* "You've got to hear this!"

In America, we tend to tell our neighbors if we get a great deal on deck furniture or find a big sale on gas grills. We would do well to strip off our sophistication, remember our own rescue, and get back to the really good news—just like our brother in Cuba or that first-century leper whom Jesus healed.

Now, what about those nine lepers who *didn't* thank Jesus? I doubt that their ungratefulness was intentional. It seems that they were so preoccupied with getting themselves to the local priest so they could be *declared* clean that they simply forgot to turn back and thank the One who *made* them clean.

Cultivating a grateful heart is not just an add-on nicety, a civil tip of the hat to God as we steamroll through *our* day. A posture of purposeful, perpetual thanks to God is absolutely central to Christian character. It gives glory to Him. It is the key defense against Satan's temptations to despair, distrust, dysfunction. It protects us from sin and self. It is the hallmark of heaven. It does not exist in hell.

As has been said, "What do praise and thanksgiving immolate and destroy? ... [Our] pride! ... That is what the extraordinary purifying power of praise consists of. Humility is concealed in praise."[6]

Satan wants to protect our precious pride from such destruction. He wants weeds of spiritual weariness and self-preoccupation in our lives. These are the first sour fruits of an ungrateful heart. But they are not the last.

Ungratefulness can become a heart-hardening habit. First comes complaining, then bitterness, anger, then feeling victimized or entitled to things that we're just not getting. Covetousness. That mindset stealthily lifts the latch and eases open the dark gate to all kinds of sin.

The apostle Paul describes the process in Romans 1. He talks about God's power and nature being clearly evident. In creation itself, God has shown us who He is. So, writes plainspoken Paul, people are without an excuse: "For although they knew God, they neither glorified Him as God nor gave thanks to him, but their thinking became futile and their foolish hearts were darkened."[7]

Ungratefulness—the refusal to glorify and thank God—is the clearest manifestation of the mother sin, human rebellion against God. It opens the gate to a slippery slope where God lets us go. From that terrifying precipice the spiritual law of gravity determines that there is no way to fall but down. "Therefore God gave them over in the sinful desires of their hearts." "God gave them over to shameful lusts." "God gave them over to a depraved mind."[8]

Ungratefulness for God's revealed character and supremacy manifests itself in all kinds of secondary sins. They all share the same root choice, the same root refusal: unwillingness to worship God as God, instead setting up the self and its own preferences as gods.

How, then, to make sure we don't slide down that slimy path? How do we immolate our pride? How do we strip off habits of ungratefulness and live in the posture of perpetual thanksgiving? Is thankfulness yet another discipline to be mastered, a daily struggle with threats of failure?

We will look at those questions in parts two and three. First, though, it's important to understand that *a grateful heart is a gift of grace*. God can make gratitude flow powerfully in our lives, like a fountain. It is actually irrepressible for those who realize that they have been rescued from torture and death—for no other reason than the undeserved kindness of God.

Some years ago, I saw an unforgettable, invigorating picture of this—when I went to Auschwitz.

CHAPTER FIVE

UNDENIABLY DELIVERED

We who lived in concentration camps can remember the men who walked through the huts comforting others, giving away their last piece of bread. They may have been few in number, but they offer sufficient proof that everything can be taken from a man but one thing: the last of the human freedoms—to choose one's attitude in any given set of circumstances.

Viktor Frankl

It was autumn when I visited Auschwitz.[1] Dead leaves skittered across the long path to its entrance; I could not quite believe I was in this notorious place. I walked past the double rows of barbed-wire fencing, the railroad tracks that transported millions to their deaths, the famous iron-arched gate with its ironic motto spelled out above: ARBEIT MACHT FREI. *Work makes freedom.*

The camp is silent now, its brick barracks a museum full of the ordinary items people brought to Auschwitz. There is a huge case of eyeglasses, another of shaving brushes and bowls; stacks of suitcases. Here is a pile of thousands of shoes, heaped on top of one another.

The shoes alone tell the tales of millions of souls. Like a pair of black high heels, half a century old but still festive. Bought for a special occasion, rarely worn, they happened to be on the feet of their owner the day the Gestapo came.

I could imagine her—call her Anna—getting off the train in Auschwitz. The knock on her door had come during dinnertime on the Sabbath. Like other Jewish families, they were to be resettled, the German officer told them. But first they would spend some time in a work camp; after all, a war was raging, and the government needed laborers.

The Germans had given Anna time to pack a small bag: some clothes, the baby's medicine, a toy for her little boy, the silver-framed photograph of her husband's parents. The soldiers told them to bring their valuables, so she had her mother's gold necklace around her neck and her diamond earrings in her bag.

Now, as she stumbled off the train holding her toddler's hand, watching her husband jump down with the baby in his arms, she shook her head. Here she was, detained for who knew how long, and she was wearing her good shoes. In the flurry of departure, she had forgotten to change. It would be a story to tell when the war was over—how she came to the work camp wobbling in high heels. Perhaps they would issue her a pair of work shoes.

But as I stood before the glass case fifty years later, I could see what happened to Anna and her shoes.

We are the shoes, we are the last witnesses.
We are the shoes from grandchildren and grandfathers
From Prague, Paris and Amsterdam,
And because we are only made of fabric and leather
And not of blood and flesh, each one of us avoided the hellfire.[2]

As they came off the train, the Jews were divided into two groups, one large, the other small. Auschwitz was already crowded with non-Jewish prisoners—Poles who had displeased their Nazi rulers. No need to make room for Jews, except for the strongest workers. Women and children were sent to one side, as were all but the most vigorous-looking men.

The large group was herded along, clutching their suitcases, to another section of the camp. A matron told them that delousing showers would be necessary. The Jews were shown where to put their belongings for retrieval later. They undressed, carefully folded their clothing and left it, with their suitcases, on a long table.

Then they walked toward the large, low building with a sign reading "BATHS." It was dug into a hill. Above its roof were plots of grass and tidy flower borders.

As the last of the large group entered the shower rooms, the doors slid shut with a metallic click. Then, through vents hidden in the grass on top of the building, Nazi orderlies dropped blue crystals into the sealed rooms below. A mist hissed from perforations in the ceilings: Zyklon B, a potent poison used to kill rodents.

The hydrogen cyanide worked quickly. The panicked victims vomited, suffocated, and emptied their bowels. Within twenty-three minutes, workers wearing gas masks and rubber boots opened the door and began unloading the corpses, a grim tangle of arms and legs.

Workers shaved the heads of the female corpses, snipped off long braids, checked for valuables, then transported the bodies to large brick ovens, where they were fed to flames so intense that they emerged as ash within the hour.

This was the fate of the owner of those high-heeled shoes I saw in the case before me. And of the child who wore the little red shoes with the broken strap and the man who owned those leather shoes, the farmer who left his boots behind, the baby who never walked in those soft blue booties . . .

I toured—if that is a word I can use—the rest of the camp. The prisoners' quarters where many non-Jewish inmates somehow survived in spite of crowding, disease, and starvation; the Wall of Death, where twenty thousand political prisoners were shot; the square where roll call was held each day; the gallows where prisoners were hanged; the barracks where perverse medical experiments were carried out on children and pregnant women; and the gas chambers themselves. The ovens are now cold, save for a single flame of remembrance.

Another memorial flame burns in a below-ground cell in Auschwitz. It honors the sacrifice of an ordinary saint ... a man whose story shows us much about the enormity of our own debt of gratitude to God.

Father Maximilian Kolbe was a Polish monk. He had founded a large Franciscan order whose headquarters was in Niepokalanow, a village near Warsaw.

Maximilian Kolbe thrilled over the budding technology of his day as a means toward world evangelism. Radio, publishing, mass media—he was dreaming of using these, without limit, to spread the Good News. Whereas St. Francis, his predecessor, had loved all living things, exclaiming his delight in "Brother Son" and "Sister Moon," Kolbe roamed through his print shop reveling in the ministry made possible by "Brother Motor" and "Sister Press."

In his simple room at the friary, he sat at a pigeonhole desk each morning, a large globe before him, praying over the world and its need for the Gospel seed. He did so tortured by the fact that a far different seed was in the air.

Nations had already fallen to Adolf Hitler and his Nazis. Storm troops marched in the streets of Austria and Czechoslovakia.

On September 1, 1939, the Nazi blitzkrieg invaded Poland; the skies filled with bombers headed for Warsaw.

Soon Niepokalanow itself was a target. Flames roared in the night and glass shattered. When the skies cleared temporarily, Father Kolbe sent many of his monks home to their families; others joined the Polish Red Cross. Thirty-six remained with Kolbe; the friary became a hospital.

In early February 1941, the Polish underground smuggled word to Kolbe that he was to be arrested. Kolbe knew what happened to the loved ones of those who tried to escape Nazi custody: their friends and families were taken instead. His church was his family—and he could not jeopardize them. So he stayed at his post.

On a morning in mid-February, Father Kolbe was sitting at his desk, praying at his globe, when he heard the sound of trucks outside his window. The Nazis had come for him.

Kolbe was found guilty of the crime of publishing unapproved materials and sentenced to Auschwitz. An SS officer informed him that the life expectancy of priests there was about a month.

By the summer, Kolbe was near death from excruciating days of hard labor. But at night he pastored his fellow prisoners in Barracks 14, praying with them, hugging their thin shoulders. Then he would raise his emaciated arm and make the sign of the cross in the foul air of the packed barracks.

"The cross!" he told them, "Christ's cross has triumphed over its enemies in every age. I believe, in the end, even in these darkest days in Poland, the cross will triumph over the swastika. I pray I can be faithful to that end."

By the end of July 1941, Auschwitz was a well-organized killing machine; the Nazis congratulated themselves on their efficiency. The camp's five chimneys never stopped smoking. The stench was terrible, and the results were horrifying: eight thousand Jews could be stripped, their possessions appropriated for the Reich, gassed, and cremated—all in twenty-four hours.

Every twenty-four hours.

The only flaw, for the Nazis, was the occasional prisoner who would figure out a way to escape. And one July night it happened. The air filled with the baying of dogs, cursing soldiers, the roar of motorcycles. A man had escaped from Barracks 14.

The next morning, after roll call in the camp yard, Camp Commandant Fritsch ordered the dismissal of all but Barracks 14. They waited. Hours passed. The summer sun beat down. Some fainted and were dragged away. Father Kolbe, by some miracle, stayed on his feet.

By evening roll call the commandant was ready to levy sentence. The other prisoners had returned from their day of slave labor; now he could make a lesson out of the fate of this miserable barracks.

The veins in Fritsch's thick neck stood out with rage. "The fugitive has not been found," he screamed. "Ten of you will die for him in the starvation bunker. Next time, twenty will be condemned."

The rows of exhausted prisoners began to sway. The starvation bunker! Anything was better—death on the gallows, a bullet in the head at the Wall of Death, or even the gas in the chambers. All those were quick, even humane, compared to Nazi starvation, for they denied you water as well as food. People didn't look like human beings after a day or two. They went mad and attacked each other, howling. They frightened even the guards. Their throats turned to paper, their brains to fire, their intestines dried like desiccated worms.

Commandant Fritsch walked the rows of prisoners. When he stopped before a man, he would command in bad Polish, "Open your mouth! Put out your tongue! Show your teeth!" So he went, choosing victims like horses.

His assistant followed behind, noting the numbers stamped on the chosen prisoners' filthy shirts. Soon there were ten men—ten numbers listed on the death roll.

The chosen groaned, sweating with fear. "My poor wife!" one man cried. "My poor children! What will they do?"

"Take off your shoes!" the commandant barked at the ten men. A pile of twenty wooden clogs made a small heap at the front of the grassy square.

Suddenly there was a commotion in the ranks. A prisoner had broken out of line, calling for the commandant. It was unheard-of to leave ranks, let alone address a Nazi officer. It was cause for execution.

Fritsch had his hand on his revolver. But instead of shooting the prisoner, he shouted at him.

"Halt! What does this Polish pig want of me?"

The other prisoners gasped. It was Father Kolbe, the priest who shared his last crust, who comforted the dying, who loved them and nourished their souls. Not Father Kolbe!

The frail priest spoke calmly to the commandant. "I would like to die in place of one of the men you condemned."

Fritsch stared at the prisoner. #16670. He never considered them as individuals; they were just a gray blur. But he looked now. #16670 didn't appear to be insane.

"Why?" snapped the commandant.

Father Kolbe knew that Fritsch never reversed an order; so he must not seem to be asking him to do so. He also knew the Nazi perspective: kill the weak and the elderly first. He was forty-six years old—but he would play on this principle.

"I am an old man, sir, and good for nothing. My life will serve no purpose."

His words triggered the response he wanted. "In whose place do you want to die?" barked Fritsch.

"For that one," Kolbe responded, pointing to the weeping prisoner who had bemoaned his wife and children.

Fritsch glanced at the other prisoner. He did look stronger than this tattered #16670 before him.

He snorted and nodded to his assistant, who drew a line through #5659 and wrote down #16670. Kolbe's place on the death ledger was set.

Father Kolbe bent down to take off his clogs. As he did so, the other prisoner passed by him at a distance—the soldiers wouldn't let them come near one another—and on the man's face was an expression so astonished that it had not yet become gratitude.

As the condemned entered Barracks 11, guards roughly pushed them down the stairs to the basement.

"Remove your clothes!" shouted an officer.

The ten naked men were herded into a dark, windowless cell.

"You will dry up like tulips," sneered the guard. He swung the heavy door shut and bolted it.

As the hours and days passed, however, the camp became aware of something extraordinary. Past prisoners had spent their dying days howling, attacking one another, clawing the walls in a frenzy of despair.

But now, coming from the death cell, those outside heard the faint sounds of singing. Hymns. Against all Nazi logic, Kolbe was leading the others gently through the valley of the shadow. And for that reason, perhaps, Father Kolbe was among the last to die.

A prisoner named Brono Borgowiec, who survived Auschwitz, served as attendant to the death cells. Each day he had to remove the corpses of those who had died.

On August 14, 1941, there were four prisoners still alive, and the bunker was needed for new occupants. A German doctor entered, four syringes in his hand. Several SS troopers and Brono Borgowiec were with him—the former to observe and the latter to carry out the bodies.

When they swung the cell door open, they saw Father Maximilian Kolbe, a living skeleton, propped against one wall. His head was inclined a bit to the left. He had the hint of a smile on his lips and his eyes wide open, fixed on some faraway vision. He did not move.

The other three prisoners were on the floor, unconscious but alive. The doctor dealt with them first: a jab of the needle into the bony left arm, a push of the piston in the syringe. It seemed a waste of the drug, but he had his orders. Then he approached #16670 and repeated the action.

In a moment, Father Kolbe was dead.

So when I visited Auschwitz, descending the basement stairs to that starvation bunker, I saw the cell at the end of the dim hallway, the place where so many died. There, on the floor, was a spray of fresh flowers, a candle burning steadily: a reminder that even in the greatest of horrors, the greatest of loves can prevail.

What if you or I had been the person for whom Maximilian Kolbe died? Would we have returned home after the war to raise

our children, live our lives, and go on our way unchanged, con-
gratulating ourselves on our good fortune? Would we forget that we'd faced death? Would we begin to
assume, over the years, that we had been spared because we'd
worked extra hard on our work detail? Such questions are ludicrous in the face of so great a deliverance. So, hopefully, we would have done what Franciszek
Gajowniczek did.

Franciszek Gajowniczek was Prisoner #5659. He survived
Auschwitz. And for fifty-three years—until his death in 1995 at
the age of ninety-five—he irrepressibly told everyone he could
about the man who had saved him. His children, grandchildren,
and their children grew up honoring Kolbe's sacrifice. During a trip
to America in 1994, Gajowniczek said that as long as he had breath
in his lungs, he would serve as a witness of Kolbe's act of love.
Anyone within a hearing radius of Gajowniczek knew the story of
his rescue. Every ordinary day for the rest of his life overflowed
with joy and thanks.

He was compelled by gratitude, like the leper who ran back to
Jesus. He was filled with joy, overcome by the gift he'd received.
Undeniably delivered from torture and death, he could do no less.

PART TWO

Removing the Obstacles

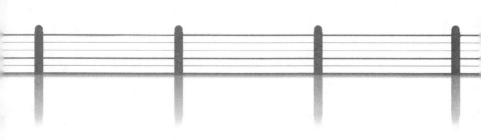

CHAPTER SIX

MY WAY—
OR THE HIGH WAY?

Beware of refusing to go to the funeral of your own independence.

Oswald Chambers

And it will be said:
"Build up, build up, prepare the road!
    Remove the obstacles out of the way of my people."
For this is what the high and lofty One says—
    he who lives forever, whose name is holy:
"I live in a high and holy place,
    but also with him who is contrite and lowly in spirit,
to revive the spirit of the lowly
    and to revive the heart of the contrite."

Isaiah 57:14–15

W hy *not* be the one? What obstacles block us from joyfully thanking God for our own rescue, like Franciszek Gajowniczek,
as long as we have breath in our lungs and life in our limbs?

First, to put it in leper language, perhaps we haven't been
cleansed of that which condemned us. If we've not yet experienced
God's grace and been born again of the Spirit, if we've not yet been
rescued from sin and death and eternal damnation in the horrors
of hell ... then, yes, that would be a serious deterrent to the free

flow of gratitude. The Spirit woos, He lures us toward the wild relief of Christ's healing grace. If we haven't yet done so, why in the wide world would we not receive Him?

The second obstacle to gratitude is that we're carrying guilt that clogs our fountain's flow. More about such shame in chapters 10 and 14.

The third, one which bears examination here, is the crusty habit of focusing on ourselves rather than God.

Earlier generations called this pride. They knew it as the worst of the seven deadly sins, the evil that led to Satan's fall.

Dante wrote that Christians who were proud carried huge, crushing boulders that bent them double, so they could not lift their eyes from the ground. Having habitually looked down on others, they could not look up to see God, nor thank Him.

But old-fashioned pride goes by all kinds of other names today. Self-sufficiency. Lifestyle rights. Autonomy. Modern American culture celebrates independence; after all, we are a nation of rugged individualists, "self-made" men and women who've pulled ourselves up by our own bootstraps—whatever a bootstrap is—lustily singing "I did it *my* way" and "I've got to be *me*" as we climb the ladder.

As social critic Henry Fairlie wrote,

> "Doing one's own thing," or any of the other similar passwords of our time, such as "I'm OK, you're OK," may seem to have little Pride in them. Where is the claim to superiority in them? Do they not merely ask to be allowed to live and let live? But what we eventually find in them is an assertion of self-sufficiency—a denial of one's *need for community* with others, which is in fact a form of selfishness, since it is always accompanied by a refusal of one's *obligation of community* with others. The steps from a reasonable self-concern to an utter selfishness are short and swift.[1]

One indicator of this modern preoccupation with self is the etymology of our English word *confident*. Its Latin origins in the mid-

1500s used to be defined as "trustful, confiding: full of conviction; assured reliance on the character, ability, strength, truth of someone or something." The underlying understanding was that human beings placed their convictions in the character of Another; they relied on a truth *outside* themselves.

That definition is now listed in *Merriam-Webster* as "obsolete." The modern description is that confidence is "characterized by assurance, especially self-reliance: confidence in and exercising *one's own powers* of judgment."

The "obsolete" concept has to do with a God orientation: there is a fixed point of absolute truth outside myself, on which I can rely. Today's concept puts me right at the center, judge of the universe and all that is in it, the arbiter and measure of truth as I perceive it. I need not consult any other authority about what's right for me.

This inflexible attitude, rooted in pride, is softened by the earnest tones and tomes of pop spirituality. "Only the heart knows what's working in our lives. The heart is our authentic compass. If we consult her, the heart can tell us if we're headed in the right direction," says the immensely popular Oprah-endorsed author Sarah Ban Breathnach.[2]

But the problem with the heart is that she is wily and will quite "authentically" justify adultery and any number of other selfish sins if we let her. And if an entire nation of people all consult their relative inner compasses, rather than navigating by fixed truth, many will sincerely arrive at vastly different conclusions from one another as to what the "right direction"—or the common good—really is.

For example, an article called "What's Right for Me" on the Proud Parenting website chronicles a high-school girl's concern that her mother and Mom's lesbian partner would look askance on her desire to date boys rather than girls. But she is relieved to find that they are quite accepting of alternative lifestyles, like being straight. Here's an excerpt.

"Amy," my mother began, "we've always tried to teach you that there is no 'right' way, no one way that fits all people. The only 'right' way to be is the one that's right for you."

"And we'll be happy for you no matter who you like," Shelley added. "Especially if that person likes you back."

I glanced around the table, at the three of us all clasping hands, forming a circle of family around our kitchen table.

"You really don't care that the person I like is a boy?" I asked.

"Of course not," my mom answered. "As long as he's a good person."[3]

The problem with this kind of subjective thinking is that it is illogical. Disavowing absolutes by definition disavows any common criteria by which to assess if someone is a "good person" or not. What if Amy's date decides that what's "right" for him is to beat women? Amy's mom has no grounds to protest that abuse is bad.

Renouncing any higher authority than the self means that people are at the mercy of any other self who happens to be stronger than they are. There is no protection for the weak.

Further, if we center on the self, we're also at the mercy of our own pride. Over the last few years the headlines have been full of business executives indicted for cheating their shareholders and breaking federal laws to further their own gains. Surrounded by sycophants, living in luxury, they lost any sense of accountability. They started to think of themselves as above the law.

As one report put it when domestic maven Martha Stewart was found guilty of obstruction of justice, "The ancient Greeks called it *hubris*, that wanton insolence or arrogance resulting from excessive pride or passion. Martha Stewart was both the victim and master of the classic temptation of mortals who, when finding themselves at the pinnacle of success, start imagining themselves bulletproofed against disaster and continue to tempt the fates."[4]

This kind of pride is not relegated to those who've been convicted or those without convictions. It slides into Christian circles quite easily, particularly among believers in comfortable circumstances. We can subtly start to believe that God is blessing us because we deserve such favor. We can end up commending Him on His good taste in connecting with us, our pride blocking the wonder and liberty of real gratitude. As Jonathan Edwards put it, "Having formed in their minds such a God as suits them, and thinking God to be such a one as themselves, who favors and agrees with them, they may like Him very well, and feel a sort of love to Him, but they are far from loving the true God."[5]

A *Harvard Business Review* article identified four characteristics of leaders who fail. They become *authoritarian*, controlling others, demanding, not willing to flex, adapt, or listen to others' input. They become *autonomous*, aloof, alone, with few relationships and little accountability. Unsurprisingly, they become *arrogant*, feeling superior and critical of others. When challenged, they rely on shame, guilt, and fear to intimidate others. And fourth, they often commit *adultery*, and their personal lives end up wreaking havoc on their corporate or political leadership.

Though believers claim a higher authority, we do the same thing. Dr. J. Robert Clinton, Professor of Leadership at Fuller Theological Seminary, has studied over five hundred Christian leaders and their experiences over a lifetime. Dr. Clinton finds many intriguing principles, all quite helpful, some quite sobering. Slightly less than one third of religious leaders "finish well." Seventy percent end up being compromised in one way or another. Sexual, family, and financial fiascoes derail many, and such "secondary" failures usually stem from the root issue of pride. These leaders rarely subject themselves to accountability or critique. They blame others for problems and abuse their power by manipulating their subordinates. They justify and deny their behavior, blinding themselves to the problems that eventually topple them and the ministries they led.[6]

Pride isolates people from one another and from God. It is, as C. S. Lewis put it, the "anti-God" state of mind. It is mutually exclusive with gratitude, for cultivating a thankful heart is not about autonomy, self-sufficiency, and self-congratulation, but dependence and thanks to Another. We perceive each day's experiences as gifts given, or opportunities allowed, by a Giver's sovereign purpose. Subverting our own will to His, we thank Him in all things. Gratitude to God is the manifestation of the fact that we rely on Him and trust Him, whatever comes. And it requires that we acknowledge we have needs, needs only He can fill.

That sounds awful to twenty-first-century ears. So, as we've seen, followers of Christ can easily acquiesce to the autonomous self-sufficiency that defines post-Christian culture. We can slide into a lifestyle that is nominally Christian, but in fact has more to do with the world's values than the Kingdom of God.

Henri Nouwen commented on this after he left the ministry fast track to weave his life with those in a community of the developmentally disabled. "When you look at today's Church, it is easy to see the prevalence of individualism among ministers and priests," he said. "... Stardom and individual heroism, which are such obvious aspects of our competitive society, are not at all alien to the Church. There too the dominant image is that of the self-made man or woman who can do it all alone."[7]

In the end, our heart reveals the reality of our worldview. Our habitual gratitude—or lack thereof—shows what we *actually* believe, not just the nice tenets we may acknowledge intellectually, but do not practice in everyday life.

Satan constantly tempts us to think of ourselves as spiritually self-sufficient and to deny the sufficiency of Christ. Even when we know full well, intellectually, that we're saved by His grace, it's so easy to strive each day to be sanctified by works. At the heart of it, it's quite difficult for us to rest on grace alone. So we add on: *Jesus plus my achievements ... Jesus plus my career success ... my well-adjusted, successful children ... my good works at church and in the community ...*

The biggest obstacle to gratitude is refusing to admit that apart from Christ, we can do nothing. We are dependent on Him. All our lives, we will have needs that we cannot fulfill by ourselves.[8]

Paradoxically, this way of dependence is not slavish. In it we find real, rollicking freedom.

So how do we slough off pride—and all those layers of sin and self-sufficiency that block us from thanking and praising God?

We can't. We need to be stripped—by Another.

CHAPTER SEVEN

GETTING NAKED

Nothing in my hand I bring,
Simply to Thy cross I cling;
Naked, come to Thee for dress;
Helpless, look to Thee for grace;
Foul, I to the Fountain fly;
Wash me, Savior, or I die.

Augustus M. Toplady, 1776

In the summer I hunger for fresh paint. Blue skies, red water-melon, good green of the fresh-cut lawn: they call me to color my house. Propelled to Home Depot, I pluck fistfuls of paint chips from the sample racks and explore the "oops" paint: cans of colors mistakenly mixed with a drop too much of this or that, and now they're free, or you can get a gallon of premium Ralph Lauren satin for a dollar. Never mind that the color can never be created again this side of eternity. What a deal!

Sometimes I paint walls. Once I couldn't help myself and painted the front door a bright, glossy purple, just to see what Lee would say when he arrived home from work that evening. (I repainted it the next day.) Sometimes I find an old piece of furniture at a neighbor's garage sale, or in the trash, or from the mysterious trove in our basement. I set the small chair or table like a sacrificial animal in the center of the paint-spattered tarp in the garage. It waits uncertainly on wobbly legs while I pull out my electric sander, rags, solvents, and brushes.

Last summer I found a side table that had potential. After using a stripping compound that removes layers of ancient paint and varnish, I sanded away every speck of residue. I carefully applied several coats of paint on the table's naked surface, then selectively sanded again for that tasteful, weathered look designers call "shabby chic."

This took hours of labor and several days of waiting for various coats of paint to dry. And I am a person who does not care for process. I want instant results. But I patiently endured the procedure because after all, it was summer, and summer is all about living at a different pace than the productive hurry of, say, September.

In the end, however, as I regarded my little table—a loving work of art painstakingly rendered over time—there was a problem. It looked terrible.

"No, no, it's fine," I told myself reassuringly. "The weathered look is supposed to look awful. That's part of its shabby charm!"

But it's better to call a spade a spade; no use bobbing and weaving in the desperate dance of denial. I had to face the disheartening reality that my hours of careful work had, in fact, been in vain.

About the time I was arriving at this painful truth, my entrepreneurial children decided to open a lemonade stand in the driveway. They made large signs and mixed pitchers of very sweet lemonade. They pulled out chairs and a beach umbrella and of course quickly incorporated as a for-profit organization with the proper tax filings.

At this point my shabby table was in the driveway in front of the open garage entrance; our big, white Chevy Suburban was behind it. The kids needed more room at the end of the driveway, near the sidewalk. They asked if I could move the car forward a little bit, toward the garage.

Still pondering my creative problem, I got in the Suburban. The little table was a few feet in front of it. But I did not move my work of bad art. Instead, I turned the key in the ignition, lightly pressed the accelerator, and drove over it.

And then I felt much better.

Fortunately, God is far more gracious with His creations.

As I've inhaled paint fumes and reflected on spiritual truths in my garage, I've thought about the things that block us from radical gratitude. Pride and other forms of sin are like layers of sludge and grime. They separate us from a clean relationship with Christ. They clog the flow of grace; they hinder the habit of thankfulness.

In this we're all like old pieces of furniture. We need to be stripped of the pride and grime that mar our design.

In the beginning, human beings were lovingly made by our Creator, crafted with clear purpose and clean lines. But sin dents, nicks, burns, stains. We ended up far from Home, in the garbage, on the curb, sitting in the dark display window of some dusty pawn shop. God found us, wherever we were. At great price, He redeemed us. We are twice His: He made us, and He bought us back.

Yet as believers, we still sin. We build up layers of dirt, unconfessed sludge, fears, and shame. We coat ourselves with pride, polish, and faux finishes—human accomplishments that we think make us look good to others. And perhaps we do look glossy—but only from a distance. Draw close and it's obvious that the sheen is only on the surface. The integrity of the creation, as designed by its Maker, has been obscured by the stuff we swathe ourselves in.

God intended for us to shine, to reflect His light, the "knowledge of the glory of God in the face of Christ," as the apostle Paul put it.[1]

But to reflect Christ's light, to live in connection with Him, we must be clean. No thick layers of repetitive sins that we just won't relinquish. No tough gloss of polyurethane so others won't see how we really are, down deep. No veneers of works we do because they make us feel worthy and just fine, thank you.

Revelation 3 speaks to this. The apostle John was writing to a wealthy group of believers in Laodicea, an ancient city known for its banking institutions, textile industries, and a medical center that produced, among other things, eye salve. In the beginnings of their church, the believers there had acknowledged their aching need for a Savior and embraced the Gospel with passion.

But gradually, their wealth had lulled them. They had no real physical needs; they drifted into an illusion that they had no spiritual needs. One can imagine their 11:00 worship service, all those well-to-do doctors, bankers, and businessmen and women, adjusting their rich robes and eyeing one another's leather footwear and designer finery. Perhaps they gathered for brunch in their richly appointed fellowship hall, laughing idly over pots of lamb stew while the world outside went to hell right around them. The comfortable Laodiceans would fit right in to many an upscale church in North America today. They had not denied Christ. But they did not seem to think they really needed Him either.

Here is what Christ said to these tepid believers:

> You say, "I am rich; I have acquired wealth and do not need a thing." But you do not realize that you are wretched, pitiful, poor, blind and naked. I counsel you to buy from me gold refined in the fire, so you can become rich; and white clothes to wear, so you can cover your shameful nakedness; and salve to put on your eyes, so you can see.[2]

But does Christ write off and reject the ones He reprimands so severely here? Are we too far gone? Far from it. "Those whom I love I rebuke and discipline," He says. "So be earnest, and repent."[3]

The passage goes on with the well-known image of Christ standing at the door, knocking. The picture is often used evangelistically, a metaphor inviting nonbelievers to open the doors of their hearts to Jesus. But this Scripture was written to *believers*.

In his odd short story "The Shoddy Lands," C. S. Lewis writes about a self-absorbed woman who has walled herself from the invasion of real love. The story's narrator hears someone knocking on her heart, "soft but unendurably heavy, as if at each blow some enormous hand fell on the outside of the Shoddy Sky and covered it completely. And with that knocking came a voice at whose sound my bones turned to water: 'Child, child, child, let me in before the night comes.' "[4]

Before the night comes . . . it is a call of alarming clarity: If we want to fellowship with Jesus, to remain in Him, to be plugged into Him, to freely feast with Him, we must hear Him and fling open the door. We must be earnest and repent. We must admit our desperate, continual need for a Savior. Not just at the point of our salvation, but every day along our sanctifying journey toward heaven.

It's a call to strip.

This is terrifyingly vulnerable for people who like to be clothed, competent, and in control. Like all of us.

But Christianity was never about self-sufficiency. It is about *God's* sufficiency and, to follow the metaphor, our inability to dress apart from Him. And when we admit our need and get naked with God, He clothes us. When we humble ourselves, He lifts us up. When we declare our desperate hunger, He welcomes us to His daily feast.

Pondering these strange and wonderful things in my garage, I've been struck by the instructions on the stripping compound can. If you read them with spiritual eyes, they become a metaphor for the process of God's discipline, in which we admit our need and repent of our sin, and He strips and cleanses us.

"Use product on upright surfaces," the label tells us. This kind of stripping is for the upright, as the Psalms call those who belong to God.

"Protect work from strong breezes. Observe precautions." God guards us from the winds of this world even as He removes our callused layers.

"Shake container well, brush on heavy coating of remover. Allow enough time for remover to work. Scrape test to be sure finish is completely softened." God shakes us up, and over time, allows the pain of scrapes in our lives to soften our hearts.

"If necessary, reapply remover and retest. Thick finishes may need several applications. Heavy sludge is best removed with a wooden scraper. Wash off remaining residue with stiff brushes or coarse rags using mineral spirits or a strong solution of other heavy duty cleaner in hot water." Some of us are stubborn. It takes more pain, more hot water, the strong solution of the Holy Spirit for us to be stripped and cleansed of the things we cling to rather than Christ.

"Before refinishing, surfaces must be clean and dry. Slightly sand dry surface. If sandpaper clogs or gums up, surface is not clean." God takes us to the end of ourselves . . . and then He gently builds us up again, clean and true, in Him.

Now, stripping compounds are just household products. They don't quite show up in the Scriptures. But the potent practice of stripping appears throughout the Bible.

The Old Testament uses severe references to the covenant people of God being stripped of jewels acquired by taking on the values of the pagan cultures around them, stripped of clothing, their fields stripped by locusts as punishment for following false gods.

In Isaiah 32, God says, "Tremble, you women who are so at ease, and hear My voice. Give ear to My word, you complacent daughters; strip, undress, and put sackcloth on your waist . . ."[5]

"I supplied all their needs," the Lord says in Jeremiah, "but they have forsaken me and sworn by gods that are not gods. Go through Israel's vineyards and ravage them." God concludes, "But do not destroy them completely. Strip off [Israel's] branches . . ."[6]

The writer of Hebrews says, "Let us strip off every weight that slows us down, especially the sin that so easily hinders our progress. And let us run with endurance the race that God has set before us."[7]

For the seeker, the new believer, or the long-time follower of Jesus, stripping is about repentance. Its key is a daily *willingness* on our part to let God have His way with us, to remove the things that block us from giving thanks to Him, to purge our impurities, whatever it takes.

One of my favorite pictures of stripping is from C. S. Lewis's *Voyage of the Dawn Treader*. Eustace, a boy whose pride and greed have caused him to inconveniently become a dragon, meets Aslan, the great Lion and Christ figure of *The Chronicles of Narnia*. Eustace is in great pain, his dragon leg constricted by a stolen golden bracelet that is cutting into his flesh. Aslan leads him to a garden on top of a tall mountain. In the center there is a wide marble well with steps going down into it. It is bubbling with cool, refreshing water, and Eustace longs to bathe his aching leg in it.

The Lion tells him he must undress before he can enter the bath. Eustace starts to respond that he can't, he's a dragon and has no clothes. But then he remembers that dragons, like snakes, can cast their skins. So he scratches himself, and individual scales start coming off. Then he digs a little deeper. His entire skin starts peeling away as a whole. He steps out of it, thinking that the dark, knobbly skin looks rather nasty.

But as he starts to step into the cool water, he sees that his foot is as hard, rough, wrinkled, and scaly as before. He scratches and tears again, and emerges from a deeper layer of ugly scales. He leaves it on the grass and goes to the well.

But it happens again. More scales, another revolting layer; he scratches and steps out of a third skin. But all his efforts are still no good. He is still a dragon. He feels hopeless. Then the Lion speaks. "You will have to let me undress you," he tells Eustace.

> "I was afraid of his claws," Eustace says, "... but I was pretty nearly desperate now. So I just lay flat down on my back to let him do it.
>
> "The very first tear he made was so deep that I thought it had gone right into my heart. And when he began pulling the skin off, it hurt worse than anything I've ever felt. The only thing that made me able to bear it was just the pleasure of feel-

ing the stuff peel off. You know—if you've ever picked the scab of a sore place. It hurts like billy-oh but it *is* such fun to see it coming away. . . .

"Well, he peeled the beastly stuff right off—just as I thought I'd done it myself the other three times, only they hadn't hurt—and there it was lying on the grass: only ever so much thicker, and darker, and more knobbly looking than the others had been. And there was I as smooth and soft as a peeled switch and smaller than I had been. Then he caught hold of me—I didn't like that much for I was very tender underneath now that I'd no skin on—and threw me into the water. It smarted like anything but only for a moment. After that it became perfectly delicious and as soon as I started swimming and splashing I found that all the pain had gone from my arm. And then I saw why. I'd turned into a boy again."[8]

As Eustace's story shows, stripping hurts. So of course we can't do it properly to ourselves. We can't go deep enough. We don't like to expose ourselves to that kind of pain. Even though we long to be freed, we'll limp along, compensating any way we can rather than allow God to remove our dragon layers.

How many of us have tolerated years of unnecessary grief to avoid what we perceive as the greater pain of shedding our snaky skins?

A friend who is addicted to alcohol told me how he wasted years by doing everything *but* dealing with his central problem. He compensated by working harder in his job. He isolated himself from friends and withdrew from his church fellowship. He engaged in endless compromises: "I'll only drink on the weekends. I'll only drink during the week. I'll only have four drinks a day. I'll only drink when I feel particularly stressed, or only on days of the week with a 'd' in their name . . ." his became a tortured life of endless compensation, particularly as it took more and more alcohol to get him drunk. Before he admitted his problem and asked for help outside himself, he was a slave. When he revealed his need, he felt absolutely naked, vulnerable. He was also set free.

" 'Come unto Me.' When you hear those words you will know that something must happen in you before you can come," says Oswald Chambers. "The Holy Spirit will show you what you have to do, anything at all that will put the axe at the root of the thing which is preventing you from getting through. You will never get further until you are willing to do that one thing. The Holy Spirit will locate the one impregnable thing in you, but He cannot budge it unless you are willing to let Him."[9]

Whoever we are, wherever we are, we can be assured of the uncomfortable news that, yes, the Holy Spirit will locate that one impregnable thing in us, that one thing that we hold on to instead of Christ alone. For some, like my friend, it is a consuming addiction. For others, it is some other form of sin, rebellion, fear, or self-sufficiency that makes us proud and keeps us cool to Christ.

For others, it can be something benign that ever so subtly detours our affections from Him. The most severe example of this that I've ever heard came from a conversation with Marty Jenco, a brother who was kidnapped, bound, gagged, and held hostage by Islamic extremists for a year and a half.

CHAPTER EIGHT

OUT OF BOUNDS

The healing path must pass through the desert, or else our healing
will be the product of our own will and wisdom. It is in the silence
of the desert that we hear our dependence upon noise. It is in the poverty
of the desert that we see clearly our attachments to the trinkets and
baubles we cling to for security and pleasure. The desert shatters the soul's
arrogance and leaves body and soul crying out in thirst and hunger.
In the desert we trust God or we die.

Dan Allender, *The Healing Path*

It began one morning at the intersection of two busy streets in
Beirut.[1]

"That's strange," Marty Jenco said to his Lebanese driver as
they waited for other cars to pass. "The policemen are standing on
the corner talking, while a grocer in a white apron directs traffic."

A moment later came the crash of automatic weapons fire.
Jenco saw men rushing his car. He heard explosions behind the
vehicle and whipped around to see more men firing their weapons
into the air. Students, parents who had been walking their children
to school, merchants—all were fleeing, terrified.

"Khaled!" Jenco yelled to his driver, suddenly understanding
what was happening. "I'm going to be kidnapped!"

Two men yanked open the car doors, shoved Jenco and Khaled
into the back, and pushed in next to them. Three others climbed in

the front, slammed the doors, and the car sped away down the now-empty street. The four policemen had vanished.

The car raced to a quiet avenue next to the sea. The men forced Khaled out and locked him in the trunk. Kalashnikovs in hand, they hustled Jenco into a second vehicle and sped away. A few miles later, they stopped, pulled him out, the guns trained on his head, and threw him in the trunk. As they did, his heavy silver cross fell from his neck. One of the men picked it up. Jenco never saw it again.

It was January 8, 1984. Father Lawrence Martin Jenco was program director for Catholic Relief Services in Lebanon. Once the seaside Paris of the Mediterranean, Beirut was now torn by civil war and violence between people of different religious, cultural, and ethnic backgrounds. The city was a maze of gun emplacements, armed checkpoints, and patrolling militiamen, with no one military or political force in control. Bombings, assassinations, and kidnappings were common.

Marty Jenco wasn't part of the region's power struggle. He oversaw the distribution of food, clothing, and medicine for people caught in the crossfire. Now he was caught himself, a prisoner of the Islamic jihad—and would remain so for the next 564 days.

"You are dead," said the young Muslim guard. Jenco was blindfolded and dragged outdoors. He could hear people talking and the pounding of nails hammered into wood. His coffin.

A voice told him to stand up. "Put your arms to your sides," the man barked. "Your legs and ankles, as close as you can get them!"

Father Jenco stood, helpless. His captors began wrapping his body with wide packing tape. A small button had popped off Father Jenco's coat earlier; now he held it tight. Focusing his attention on the button helped to relieve his rising tide of panic.

The men wound the tape around his legs, torso, shoulders, neck. "Open your mouth!" one commanded. They stuffed in a piece of cloth, taped his mouth shut, then wrapped the rest of his head, leaving only his nostrils exposed.

The men slid him like a mummy under the bed of a truck, into the space where spare tires are stored. He heard a metal door close. "They've wrapped my body for burial," he thought, "and put me in a hearse."

It was sweltering, the exhaust fumes so overwhelming that Father Jenco could hardly breathe. At every bump in the road his body jolted, battering his taped face against the hot metal. The blood coagulated in his nasal passages, making it even harder for him to get air. Occasionally the truck would stop, engine running. Military checkpoints.

Father Jenco clutched the button in his helpless hand and repeated the ancient prayer: "Lord Jesus, Son of God, have mercy on me, a sinner." Focusing on Jesus, breath after ragged breath, he developed a rhythm in his breathing; peace overruled his panic.

For the next year and a half, Marty Jenco was held in a succession of tiny rooms, spirited like a mummy to hiding places outside of Beirut in order to evade authorities. He was used as a political pawn, became an inadvertent international celebrity, suffered countless indignities at the hands of his captors.

Early in his captivity another hostage, Jeremy Levin of CNN, escaped. Other prisoners were taken. One night he heard whispers in the dark.

"Who are you?"

"I am Ben Weir," said a voice. "I'm a Presbyterian minister. Who are you?"

"I am William Buckley," said another. "I am an American diplomat from the embassy in Beirut."

William Buckley was, in fact, a CIA officer. His remains would later be found on a roadside near the Beirut airport.

There were others. Terry Anderson, Associated Press bureau chief. David Jacobson, administrator of American University Hospital. Tom Sutherland, a dean of American University of Beirut.

These men were eventually chained in the same room with Father Jenco. They shared one filthy towel, one occasional tub of tepid water. They would bathe in it, consecutively. Eventually they all agreed that they were glad they were not married to any of the others.

Occasionally their captors let them listen to a radio. They heard President Reagan's challenges to the Soviet Union. They grieved over the explosion of the space shuttle Challenger. They heard the voices of their family members pleading for their release.

Like the others, Jenco was blindfolded much of the time. His infected eyes started oozing and crusting. The terrorists kidnapped a Lebanese Jewish doctor, who prescribed Terramycin. The young guards religiously applied the ointment to Jenco's diseased eyes.

The doctor also prescribed medication for Jenco's skyrocketing blood pressure. It too was bought and given to him.

Later, his captors executed the doctor.

Jenco was allowed to use the bathroom once a day. He was fed on the floor. "I am not an animal!" he shouted to his captors. "I am a human being!"

The guards probed his mouth. "Those!" they shouted, pointing to his dental fillings. "You are CIA! Those are transmitters!" Over the months he was beaten, kicked, shoved, spun, pistols shoved in his face, clubbed, wrapped with plastic explosives, then told they were duds.

Eventually, meditating in a corner, on the floor, Father Jenco remembered the words of Philippians 4. He made them his own.

> The Lord is near, Marty. Dismiss all anxiety from your mind. Present your needs to God in every form of prayer and in petitions full of gratitude.

He did.

> Then God's own peace, which is beyond all understanding, will stand guard over your heart and mind in Christ Jesus.

And it did.

So in the end, Marty Jenco found that he was actually guarded by God's peace—not the young soldiers of Hezbollah.

Father Jenco's captors released him on July 26, 1985. His family met him at the U.S. air base in Germany that became the setting for so many hostage-family reunions in the 1980s. He met with President Reagan at the White House and with Pope John Paul II at the Vatican. There was a parade in his Indiana hometown. And he worked hard for the release of his brother hostages.

When I met with Father Jenco in 1989, he spoke powerfully about his imprisonment and its spiritual lessons. I was overwhelmed by the fact that this gentle priest could practice the art of gratitude while imprisoned by terrorists. If he could do that in such horror, I thought, certainly I can do it in my everyday life.

But then he told me another part of his story. It relayed, even more viscerally, the deep, deep love of God—and His relentless call that we be stripped of all but the Lord Jesus.

Father Jenco's worst tortures were the transports. He dreaded the claustrophobic panic of being wrapped like a corpse and stuffed in the undercarriage of a truck. It strained his unstable heart.

But because of his focus on Jesus—and the comfort of the meditative button in his clenched hand—he got through it each time.

"That button became very important to me," he said. "I needed it. If I misplaced it, I would search madly for it. It was a security."

But eventually, he sensed the Holy Spirit locating what Oswald Chambers calls that "one impregnable thing." As he prayed, thought, meditated, it was inescapable. Father Jenco knew that God was telling him this: *I am with you always . . . even when you are bound and gagged and stuffed under a truck. So next time they move you, I want you to let go of the button.*

At this point as Father Jenco related his story, I grabbed his arm, aghast, my eyebrows up. "Oh, God," I thought. "He'd been through so much! Why couldn't the button be out of bounds? Please, just let him have the button!"

But no. There was a massive spiritual principle at work in this humble priest. And in the horrors of captivity, his faith wasn't about Jesus plus anything. Not even Jesus plus a nice, innocuous little button.

He let go, and threw it away.

And the next time his captors hauled him out to be bound, gagged, and thrown into the dark, Father Jenco's hands weren't clenched, but open, his empty palms up in a gesture of submission ... or worship, for those who had eyes to see.

Marty Jenco died in 1996. He fought the good fight. His race is run, done, and he is with his Savior.

What's *your* button?

CHAPTER NINE

LETTING GO

Those who cling to worthless idols forfeit the grace that could be theirs.
—Jonah 2:8

...the new sort of life will be spreading through our system, because now
we are letting Him work at the right part of us. It is the difference between
paint, which is merely laid on the surface, and a dye or stain which soaks
right through.... [Christ] never talked vague, idealistic gas. When he said,
"Be perfect" He meant it. He meant that we must go in for the full
treatment. It is hard; but the sort of compromise we are all hankering after
is harder—in fact, it is impossible. It may be hard for an egg to turn into
a bird: it would be a jolly sight harder for it to learn to fly while remaining
an egg. We are like eggs at present. And you cannot go on indefinitely
being just an ordinary, decent egg. We must be hatched or go bad.

C. S. Lewis

As with Marty Jenco, the "one impregnable thing" we clutch so
tight can be as light as a button—something so innocuous that
no one else would think twice about it. But we know it preoccupies
our affections. Inside, we know that our confidence is not in Christ
alone, nor are we thanking Him for *His* sufficiency to meet our needs.

Or the one thing that hinders can be as heavy as the chains of
a sinister and secret sin. If anyone else found out what we fondle
in the hidden places of our hearts, we would shrivel and die of
shame.

Either way, we come to the point in the journey where we can go no further. We must deal with it. And whether we bear the invisible yoke of secret sin, or simply clutch a nice crutch that no one would question, each of us knows what holds us back. Letting go of what we treasure—whether it is foul or fair, loathsome or lovely—is a radical and vulnerable choice.

But just beyond that choice lies liberation.

Father Jenco took the plunge when he threw away that little button. He was still a captive. But he was free.

Perhaps more of us can relate to Eustace's story from the Chronicles of Narnia. We cannot strip ourselves of the things that bind. We must submit to the Lion's claws. But He will not remove our scaly layers and hard hearts without permission. We must be *willing* to be stripped, to surrender our defenses, to let God have His way with us.

For me, the story that nails this principle of willingness comes from Corrie ten Boom. Many years ago, Corrie came to our church one Sunday evening. The sanctuary was packed with people waiting to hear the stories of this elderly saint. She spoke about the topics so familiar to readers of her books: how the ten Boom family hid Jews from the Nazis during World War II, their arrest and the deaths of most of them in the concentration camps, her survival and subsequent ministry.

Corrie ten Boom spoke of a crossroads in her own journey with Jesus. After World War II, she went to many churches in Europe, preaching the Gospel and a powerful message of forgiveness. "When we confess our sins," she would say, "God casts them into the deepest ocean, gone forever."[1]

After one such service in a church in Germany, a man came to Corrie.

"A wonderful message, Fräulein!" he said.

She recognized him immediately. He had been a guard at Ravensbrück, the concentration camp where she had been held and her sister had died. She remembered a stark room there, bright, harsh lights, a pile of dresses and shoes in the center of the floor, and the shame of walking naked past this man. She remembered the leather crop that had hung from his belt, the visored cap with its skull and crossbones. She remembered his sadism and cruelties. But he did not remember her.

"How good it is to know that, as you say, all our sins are at the bottom of the sea!" he continued. "You mentioned Ravensbrück . . . I was a guard there. But since that time, I have become a Christian. I know that God has forgiven me for the cruel things I did there, but I would like to hear it from your lips as well. Fräulein, will you forgive me?"

He stood there, his hand extended, a former Nazi asking pardon of a former victim.

"I stood there," Corrie ten Boom said years later, "I, whose sins had again and again been forgiven—and could not forgive."

She remembered her sister . . . could Betsie's slow, terrible death be erased simply for the asking?

It couldn't have been very long that the man remained with his hand stuck out, but to Corrie it seemed hours, for she was wrestling with the most difficult thing she'd ever had to do. She thought of Jesus' words: "If you do not forgive men their sins, your Father will not forgive your sins."[2]

She knew, too, that since the war, Holocaust victims who had forgiven their enemies had been able to rebuild their lives. Those who had remained bitter had remained invalids. It was as simple and as horrible as that.

Corrie's heart was frozen. But she knew that forgiveness is not an emotion. It is an act of the will. She also knew that the will can function regardless of the temperature of the heart.

"Jesus, help me!" she prayed silently. She knew she could not forgive. "I can lift my hand. I can do that much. *You* supply the feeling."

Mechanically, she did what she could. She lifted her arm and stuck her hand into the man's outstretched one.

"As I did," she said, "an incredible thing took place. The current started in my shoulder, raced down my arm, sprang into our joined hands. And then this healing warmth seemed to flood my whole being, bringing tears to my eyes."

"I forgive you, brother!" she shouted. "With all my heart!"

Though Corrie's story is an amazing example of forgiveness, the key principle here involves the interaction between her will and God's power. It applies to any of us.

Certainly God could override our wills and make us holy robots. But in His divine pleasure, rooted in paradox, He wants free servants, not programmed slaves. No Stepford Christians. He revels in those who obey Him out of love and gratitude, who are earnest to forgive as they have been forgiven. And He is on the case: when we show even a shred of faith, the smallest action of obedience, He'll bring us the rest of the way. For Corrie ten Boom, He didn't demand that she manufacture an emotion that she could not. He nudged her to *do what she could: just lift that arm.* He did the rest.

Willingness is expressed in obedient action, however small. Lift your arm. Toss the button. Make the call. Admit the truth. When we come to the sticking point, we must do something, even if it feels impossible.

Jesus spoke of this in His story of the errant son who had scorned his home, wasted his father's money, and gone as far as first-century sex, drugs, and rock-and-roll could take him. No innocent victim like Corrie ten Boom, he was in a pigpen mess of his own making. But he came to his senses. To enjoy the riches of his father's house, he knew he had to get up and head home. "I will arise and go to my father," he determined.[3]

Realizing what we need to do is one thing. Doing it is another. Taking action is hard, even in settings that stink. We don't know how long the prodigal remained in the mud, eyeing the hog snacks and smelling of pig poop.

"I will arise," he thought again. We can be sure the Enemy was right by his side, murmuring soothingly in his ear. *Excellent idea. But you're not ready for such a drastic action yet. Surely the pigs will leave a few pods you can munch. Much better to get up tomorrow, when you're feeling stronger.*

If the prodigal had waited until he *felt* like getting up, he never would have gone home. He had to express his willingness to do the big thing—confess his wrongs to his father and admit his guilt—by doing a small thing. He had to get up.

The principle of willingness expressed through action is all over the Scriptures.

In Jesus' day a woman who had come to the end of herself came to Him. She had a physical problem, a hemorrhage that had lasted for twelve years. Older translations of the gospel of Mark call her the "woman with the issue of blood."

Even though managed health care was not her lot, her situation sounds modern. She had gone to many different doctors. She had spent everything she had. Yet instead of getting better, she had gotten worse. She had exhausted all her options.

Except one.

She had heard about Jesus. The historical account says that she thought, "If I just touch his clothes, I will be healed." We can assume that Mark knew what was in this unnamed woman's mind because she told him later, when she had become his friend and part of the community of faith.

We can imagine the scene. Her condition could have been gastrointestinal, but it was more likely a chronic menstrual or uterine disorder, endometriosis run amok. She would have been wracked by pain, drained by anemia, shaky from hormonal imbalances.

In addition to these physical ailments, she would have been bowed by shame. Old Testament rabbinical law declared that Jewish women of the day were ceremonially "impure" during the time of their menstrual flow. A woman who suffered bleeding for any other reason was to be "unclean as long as she has the discharge, just as in the days of her period."[4]

Unclean! Unclean!

She decided to do what she could, to get up and go to Jesus. She caught up with Him near the Sea of Galilee. He was surrounded by a huge crowd of people. A local synagogue leader named Jarius was leading Jesus toward his home, where his young daughter was dying. Religious officials and other important people swarmed around Christ. No one would have noticed a pale, gaunt woman following along at the edge of the crowd, except to swat her away if she got too close.

But she is determined. The swirl of robes around her, sandaled feet, clouds of dust . . . she threads her way closer to the center, her eyes on Jesus' woven cloak. "If I can just touch His clothes," she thinks. "Just the edge of His coat. The border of His robe."

Closer. Closer. Her hand is extended, reaching for the hem of God.

She is pushed to the side. She presses on. She catches the rough nub of cloth between thumb and fingers.

Power.

Jesus stopped. He had felt the healing surge rush out.

"Who touched me?"

The disciples, ever helpful, were quick to chide their master. "You see the people crowding against you," they scolded. "And yet you can ask, 'Who touched me?'"

Jesus gave them the attention they deserved. He turned away, searching for the woman . . . although He knew just where she was.

She came. She fell at His feet, trembling with fear, and told Him her story.

"Daughter, your faith has healed you," Jesus told her tenderly. "Go in peace and be freed from your suffering."[5]

Go in peace. Be freed. She hadn't figured out everything about Jesus theologically. But she had been stirred to do what she could: find Him and reach for His hem. He took her the rest of the way.

Similarly, a man who was absolutely distraught came to Jesus. His son had been ill since childhood with violent convulsions. The father's heart was broken. "If you can do anything, take pity on us and help us," he cried to Jesus.

"*'If you can'*?" Jesus repeated to him. "Everything is possible for him who believes."

Many of us would have left in despair at that point, assuming that we'd blown it, that Jesus demanded flawless faith, and that we'd have to come back another day, another decade, when we believed better. This father was at the end of himself. He cried from his very core.

"I do believe!" he exclaimed. "Help me overcome my unbelief!"

Jesus healed his son.

The principle is so tender and true. God doesn't demand that our faith be polished, perfect, muscular, macho. He just demands that we come with the raggedy faith we have.

Come.

On this issue of willingness, we can also draw great encouragement from, you guessed it, a leper.

He was covered with disease. Parts of him were missing. He was, of course, unclean.

But he came to Jesus. He fell on the ground before Him.

"Lord," he said, "if you are willing, you can make me clean."

Jesus reached out His hand. He must have smiled. He touched the man.

"I am willing," He said.

And the leper was healed.[6]

God is willing. Before He even heals and cleanses us, He's willing to connect with us in our dirty sin and bleeding brokenness. He'll touch us as we are.

The question is, are *we* willing?

CHAPTER TEN

NO REGRETS

O Lord, Thou didst strike my heart with Thy Word and I loved Thee.

St. Augustine

Like the woman with the issue of blood, we are all people with an issue. It might be a benign button or a secret sin: small or large, something that needs to be confessed, tossed, healed, stripped. If we honestly don't know what it is, God will certainly reveal anything that prevents us from full freedom and over-whelming gratitude to Him.

But most of us know. It is that thing inside about which we are even now faintly thinking, "You can have anything but *that*," or "of course it's not *that*."

Few of us could have criticized Corrie ten Boom if she had not forgiven the former Nazi tormentor. After all, she was a hero, a Holocaust survivor who had hidden Jews. She was preaching the Gospel, doing great things for the Kingdom. She was entitled to her distaste, wasn't she?

She says she was not. God had brought her to a crossroads she couldn't scoot by. Untold outcomes weighed and waited in the balance of that moment in 1947 when the former Nazi stood before her, his hand extended. Would she let go of her hatred and forgive? Or would she clutch it, rationalizing its corroding presence in her life? Would she just lift her arm—or leave it clenched?

She made her choice.

In the thirty-six years that followed before she went on to glory, did Corrie ever regret that choice? Can we imagine her taking stock before she died: "Ah, if only I hadn't pardoned that guard! How much more wonderful life would have been if I had held on to hatred and anger! Oh, I wish I hadn't forgiven!"

Similarly, did the prodigal daydream, sometimes, of starvation in the pigpen, wishing he'd never come home to his father's feast? Did the healed woman reflect fondly on her days of blood and pain, regretting the risk that healed her? In heaven, does Father Jenco wish he had his button back?

In the face of eternity, and after the new freedom that follows the choice of willingness, such questions sound absurd. It is only *before* we act and take the plunge of obedience that Satan can paralyze us with his lies of fear and self-protection.

So we must be brave and surrender, releasing anything that keeps us from real connection with Christ. In this struggle, it is the cowardly who keep fighting against the will of God. The bold and daring submit to Him, allowing themselves to be stripped of that which binds and blocks them from relying on Christ alone.

As we said in chapter 7, stripping is about repentance. As we saw in chapter 9, it starts with willingness. The next step is to consider the real nature of biblical repentance. It is far more wonderful than its caricatures would let on.

For many, the call to repent conjures up cartoon images of kooky killjoys wearing sandwich boards and shouting at harried people on the sidewalk. Even those who acknowledge the need to repent often think of it in terms of guilt, fear, shame, self-punishment, penance, and "trying to do better."

But *real* repentance is decidedly different. It gives no guilt; it leaves no regrets. It is not about working harder to be good and not mess up. Real repentance is intimate, refreshing liberation, astonishingly powerful. It is not self-centered shame, but a God-centered gift of grace. Through it, we come to saving faith in Christ in the first place. Through it we grow in a lifelong relationship with Him.

In the New Testament, "repentance" is most often translated as the Greek word *metanoia*. *Meta* means "after," *noia* "the mind," or "to think." It means a fundamental paradigm shift: an inward change of mind after the Spirit's conviction that results in godly sorrow for sin, confession of it that we might be forgiven, and a change in how we live.

Real repentance springs from God's initiative, not ours. For example, consider the apostle Peter's speech to thousands on the day of Pentecost. He spoke with passion about the Christ he had denied. But he wasn't crippled by shame. He was Exhibit A of the transforming power of repentance and forgiveness. Peter had never been particularly successful at saying more than a paragraph without putting his foot in his mouth. But now he was different.

When the people heard his words, they were cut to the heart. "What do we do?" they cried.

"Repent and be baptized," said Peter. "Every one of you, in the name of Jesus Christ for the forgiveness of your sins. And you will receive the gift of the Holy Spirit."[1]

Pierced to the core, about three thousand Jews repented and were baptized. Right then.

But this salvation wasn't just for one particular people group. Soon non-Jews believed on Jesus. This was difficult for Jews to understand, coming from their worldview of strict segregation. It was hard for Peter. But then he discovered, surprise, that God was bigger than his bias. "So if God gave them the same gift as he gave us who believed in the Lord Jesus Christ," he mused, "who was I to think that I could oppose God?"[2]

When they heard this, the church leaders also gave over their prejudices. *Whoa*, they said. *This is bigger than we thought!* "God has granted even the Gentiles repentance unto life!"[3]

This is a great picture of God's open arms to all, and the apostles' willingness to think in His terms, not their own. More than that, it's clear that *God* grants saving repentance. It's a gift.

But over the centuries after the New Testament was written, many church fathers gradually put increasing stress on *human* efforts. Accordingly, believers' lives became much more stressful. The Latin Vulgate translation of *metanoia* became *paenitentia*, which implied that acts of penance had to be done if a person hoped to receive grace. Skewed thinking became tradition: believers confessed their sins not to God, but to priests, who assigned tasks of contrition.

Then there were indulgences, a brisk business in pieces of grace that ran like a banking system. The idea was that the virtues of the saints of the past created an inexhaustible account of goodness. If your personal account had been depleted by sin's withdrawals, you could withdraw from the credit of the saints. All you had to do was view a holy relic belonging to one of them, pay the prescribed price, and your account would be credited. (Accordingly, the Church had great storehouses of relics, including such things as a strand of Jesus' beard, a piece of bread from the Last Supper, a twig from Moses' burning bush, a tooth from St. Jerome, four pieces of St. Augustine and six of St. Bernard. All could be viewed, for a price.)

The effect of all this was that fear and uncertainty reigned: will my efforts be enough to make up for my sins? Maybe if I try more, cry more, buy more? The Good News wasn't so good anymore.

The Reformers lanced the boil and peeled back the crusty layers of human tradition, returning to the heart of the Gospel. Regarding repentance, they came back to the sense of the original Greek, putting the emphasis back on God's unmerited favor, rather than human works. Martin Luther wrote that "*metanoia* signifies a changing of the mind and heart, because it seemed to indicate not only a change of heart, but also a manner of changing it, i.e., *the grace of God.*"[4]

What does repentance look like?

It looks like Zacchaeus. A tax collector, he'd become quite rich by taking fat kickbacks for himself before he turned tax monies over to the Romans. People hated him. He hated himself, bound by his own greed. But when Jesus found him, up in a tree and out on a limb, He loved Zacchaeus. That acceptance struck his heart—and he loved Jesus back.

"Here and now," he shouted, free at last, "I give half my possessions to the poor, and if I've cheated anyone, I'll pay him back with 400 percent interest!"[5]

Repentance looks like Ebenezer Scrooge on Christmas morning. So grateful to be given a second chance, rather than be damned by his deadly greed, he's in his pajamas shouting out the windows, flinging gifts to startled passersby. "I am as light as a feather, I am as happy as an angel, I am as merry as a school-boy. I am as giddy as a drunken man. A merry Christmas to everybody! A happy New Year to all the world! Hallo here! Whoop! Hallo!"[6]

After they really repent, people can barely contain themselves. They whoop. They've been set free. They are no longer the same. That is because:

First, Real Repentance Leaves No Regrets

The apostle Paul wrote a tough letter to the church at Corinth. We don't know just what they'd been up to. His communiqué hurt their feelings. But it also brought about godly change in their lives.

In 2 Corinthians, Paul writes to them again. We can imagine them opening his letter quite gingerly. He tells his Corinthian friends that he was sorry to injure them, so to speak, but that he was glad his words had led to their repentance. "For you became sorrowful as God intended and so were not harmed in any way by us," he says. "Godly sorrow brings repentance that leads to salvation and leaves no regret, but worldly sorrow brings death."[7]

Satan desperately wants us to engage in *worldly* repentance, with its cycling chains of shame, remorse, despair. Death. It keeps us focused on ourselves, on our past, refusing to believe God's radical promises. It binds plenty of Christians who could be free.

Believers still sin. If we say that we don't, we deceive ourselves. And we are to confess our sins to God. Not because He doesn't know them, but in naming them we humble ourselves, agree with

Him, and acknowledge our aching need for a Savior. When we confess, God says He will be faithful to forgive our sins and to completely cleanse us from them.[8]

Real repentance brings total cleansing. It leaves no sticky residue of regret.

Second, It Is Refreshing

When the people were "cut to the heart" on the day of Pentecost, they wanted to know what to do. The Spirit penetrates the heart; then the obedient person acts. Peter told them, "Repent, then, and turn to God, so that your sins may be wiped out, that times of refreshing may come from the Lord."

So simple, and so powerful. God wipes out our sins when we come to Him, and that tsunami of grace brings "times of refreshing."

A friend who is an ex-offender told me how, in his former life, he used to speed along the highway, a gun under his seat, drugs in his system, a string of offenses on his record. He was terrified that a police officer would pull him over and he'd be caught. Guilty.

Eventually he *was* caught. In prison, he came to know Christ and changed his ways. After he got out, he'd drive along the highway, observing the speed limit, grinning, and hoping that an officer would pull him over anyway—just so he could enjoy the fact that he had absolutely nothing to hide.

My friend relished the "times of refreshing" that real repentance brings.

Third, It Involves Radical Surgery

King David refers to this in Psalm 51. David's Hollywood-scale temptations had lured him, step by slippery step, into adultery, murder, and such terrifying layers of deceit that he couldn't even see what was apparent to everyone else. So God sent Nathan the prophet to David—and Nathan peeled the calluses off David's denial.

In his raw prayer of repentance, David cried, "Create in me a pure heart, O God, and renew a steadfast spirit within me!"[9]

Similarly, God tells His people, "I will cleanse you from all your impurities and from all your idols. I will give you a new heart and put a new spirit in you; I will remove from you your heart of stone and give you a heart of flesh."[10]

Like the biblical picture of the heart transplant, real repentance doesn't mean putting a Band-aid on the problem, denying its severity, hoping it will somehow get better and go away on its own. It means acknowledging the problem for what it really is and cutting it out.

I thought of this when I read a newspaper story about a woman named Michele who vacationed with her family in Costa Rica. They explored the rain forest, dormant volcanoes, and verdant vistas of flora and fauna. One day Michele went for a wonderful, solitary walk in the forest.

When she returned home, she noticed two red bites, one on each leg. Evidently some form of fauna had nibbled on her. The bites became inflamed. They oozed, itched, reddened, grew. Sometimes at night Michele felt deep, stabbing pains, as if "something was moving inside the bite."[11] She went to her internist, who decided they were tick bites and put her on antibiotics.

The bites continued to ooze and grow. A second doctor put her on a second antibiotic. A third physician seemed to think the problem—particularly Michele's account of severe, shifting pains at night—was all in her head.

But the bites' swollen, weeping, blue-green mounds were not in Michele's head. Another doctor looked at them sympathetically, but was flummoxed. By now two months had gone by.

Then, at the library, Michele came upon a travel book. Its chapter on insect-borne diseases caught her eye, particularly when it described her symptoms perfectly. This was reassuring . . . until she realized that the mounded infections were caused by tropical botfly larvae. In other words, she had maggots living in her legs. The book advised smearing peanut butter, Vaseline, or raw bacon on the lesions in order to suffocate the resident maggots.

Michele took a deep breath and got out the Jif. After she coated the first bite with peanut butter, a white, wormlike creature started to push through to the surface. She tried to pull it out with tweezers, but couldn't grasp it.

It was time to bring in the professionals. A dermatologist confirmed the botfly diagnosis and prepared Michele for outpatient surgery. Local anesthetic was administered to each leg. The doctor opened the first mound with a scalpel, removed things that no one wanted to look at, and then, gingerly, pulled out a white, fat, striated worm about an inch long and a quarter-inch wide. A few minutes later she removed a pale, flaccid, even larger worm from Michele's other leg.

Now, in my personal, nonscientific survey of this story's effects, no one who hears it ever forgets it. So, aside from grossing us all out approximately forever and deterring us from strolling in the rain forest, what is the point?

I'm not using Michele's story literally here, as if she needed to repent. It is simply a rather riveting medical illustration of a spiritual principle. When we don't take action, the revolting stuff inside of us grows and festers. It's painful. King David, who would know, said this: "When I kept silent [about my sin], my bones wasted away through my groaning all day long.... My strength was sapped, as in the heat of summer."[12]

Who really wants to walk around in pain, wasting away with unconfessed spiritual worms inside? Why would we not run to repent? Any pain involved in the operation is worth the freedom afterwards.

Fourth, Real Repentance Produces Fruit

John the Baptist told new converts to "produce fruit in keeping with repentance."[13]

When I started working with Chuck Colson in 1980, he was still receiving lots of letters castigating him for his role in the Nixon White House and his behaviors before he became a Christian in 1973. Many writers were deeply skeptical about his "so-called religious conversion." The kinder ones accused him of founding Prison Fellowship as a scam to pad his own pockets. (I can think of a lot more lucrative ways to do that than prison ministry.) The nastier ones were unrepeatable.

But as the years went by, the once-steady tide of those letters lessened. Antagonists may not have liked Chuck Colson any better. But it was hard to argue that his conversion was not sincere when the fruits of his repentance were so tangible. God had used Prison Fellowship's ministry to touch and change tens of thousands of prisoners. Christian offenders' recidivism rates were dramatically lower than nonbelievers' rates of return to prison for new offenses. And it was hard to argue that Chuck was somehow profiting from Prison Fellowship when he gave his book royalties and other monies—like the $1 million Templeton Prize—to the ministry.

Just as real faith reveals itself in works, real repentance reveals itself in changed behavior. No one would have believed that Scrooge or Zacchaeus or Colson had changed if their actions didn't show it.

One of the clearest negative examples of this is the eighteenth dynasty Pharaoh of Egypt who held the Israelites in slavery. Viewed by his people as descendent of the sun-god Ra, he was accustomed to getting his own way. God told Moses to confront him. Moses was not enthusiastic about the job at first, but it grew on him . . . and he obediently kept reappearing in Egypt's gilded palace, telling Pharaoh to let God's people go.

Then came the plagues, one by one. After one particularly interesting barrage of flaming hail, thunder, and lightning, Pharaoh summoned Moses.[14]

"This time I have sinned," he told him. Perhaps he'd been hit by hail. "The LORD is in the right, and I and my people are in the wrong. Pray to the LORD, for we have had enough thunder and hail. I will let you go."

Still, Pharaoh's "repentance" had a lot more to do with his ruined crops than it did with understanding God's holiness and his own sin. Moses said as much: "The thunder will stop and there will be no more hail, so you may know that the earth is the LORD's. But I know that you and your officials still do not fear the LORD God."

Moses was right. When the hail and thunder and scary stuff stopped, Pharaoh did not let the Israelites go.

Any of us can relate. We are often like children who deeply regret the *consequences* of disobedience. Given the chance, though, we'd do it again if we could just get away with it. But real repentance, that gift of God, brings the fruit of changed behavior.

Fifth, Real Repentance Normatively Takes Place in the Community of Believers

Sin and shame isolate us, not only from God, but from one another. Admitting our sins and asking God's forgiveness is first, a personal transaction of grace between an individual and God. But Christianity was never meant to be lived out in isolation. It is by definition corporate. We live our faith in the community of a local church, in real relationships with real people. Christ's love binds us together—and *friends in Him can help us live new after God refreshes us.*

Here's a picture of that.

Jesus stands outside the closed crypt of His dead friend Lazarus. A huge crowd of friends, skeptics, and onlookers surround Him. *Open the tomb*, Jesus commands. Practical Martha, the dead man's sister, is quick to remind him that her brother has been decomposing for four days now: the odor will be appalling.

Jesus tells her she's about to see a miracle.

The people pull away the heavy stone. The tomb entrance is a dark hole.

Then Jesus shouts. "Lazarus! Come out!"

Silence. The people hold their breath.

Then, an unbelievable sound: the dead man shuffles from the dark doorway. He just could not stay dead: Jesus had called him.

But he hobbles, trussed in the tight strips of linen in which the dead of his day were wrapped. His legs are bound, his body swathed, his chest, neck, even his head enveloped like a mummy . . . wait, he *was* a mummy.

Lazarus hops toward the Lord.

Jesus must have smiled.

He nudges Lazarus's friends. "Take off the grave clothes," he tells them, "and let him go!"

I can just see them getting hold of the end of the long linen strip, pulling quick, full of joy. Lazarus unspools, spinning like a top across the ground. He lands in Jesus' arms.

God heals, pardons, delivers us from death. Then He uses our friends to help strip off our stinky rags.

The key to a lifestyle of repentance without regrets is remembering that this is not a *human* endeavor. We are in a relationship with the God of the universe, not some small deity of our own making. As always, Satan would have us believe that it is all about us: *our* sin, *our* shame, *our* guilt, *our* agenda, and, most of all, *our* control. He will constantly tempt us—it's not hard—to focus downward and inward, studiously studying our navels, covered in lint, locked down to resist the holy invasion.

Meanwhile, God, who raises people from the dead, forgives us when we repent and look to Him. He wants to bear us away to new heights, blasting us clean in the waterfall of His grace.

Many believers tend to think about such forgiveness as pardon—and that is a huge concept. But it's not big enough. In Romans, the apostle Paul used the term *justified* to describe the believer's standing before God. As a child I was taught to think about that term as "just-as-if-I'd" never sinned. But I couldn't get hold of what that really meant.

Here's a picture that has helped me begin to get it.

A man has served in prison for ten years of a life sentence. He's been found guilty of a crime he doesn't even remember. During a drug-and-alcohol induced blackout one night, he killed someone. He's filled with shame and guilt, serving his sentence in a bleak maximum security prison, day after awful day.

One day a prison officer comes to his cell. "Get your stuff together," he tells the inmate. "You're getting out."

The prisoner jumps up. "What do you mean?"

"You've been pardoned," the officer tells him.

"What?" the man stutters.

"The governor pardoned you. You're free. Right now!"

The man is escorted to the front gate, given clothes, a bus ticket, and some money. He is free to start his new life.

But there's a problem. Even though he's free, he's still eaten up by guilt. Even though he's been pardoned, he's still sick with shame about the person he killed.

A second man is in prison for the exact same reason. He too was convicted of killing someone during a druggy blackout. He too is filled with remorse and shame.

One day an officer comes to this man's cell. "Get your things," he tells the inmate. "You're getting out."

The man jumps up. "What?"

"It's incredible," the officer tells him. "A guy in another state— he was on his deathbed, and he confessed to the murder, after all these years. They did DNA tests. You're totally cleared. He did it. Not you!"

The inmate is escorted to the front gate, given clothes, a bus ticket, and some money. He's free to start his new life.

Is he eaten up by guilt?

No. *He didn't commit the crime.* He's innocent. And so he is really free.

This story is not literal. As sinners, we *are* truly guilty. But the picture of justification is accurate. Jesus paid for our sins at the cross, and the Bible says that we are justified. Not guilty after all! Because of Jesus' perfect righteousness, God looks at us just as if we had never sinned, as if we had never broken His law. He judges that we are *innocent*.

That's why real repentance, with God's radical promise of forgiveness, removes obstacles from our path. It sets us free indeed, puts springs in our step, and fills our fountains with fresh-flowing gratitude.

PART THREE

THE BIG PICTURE

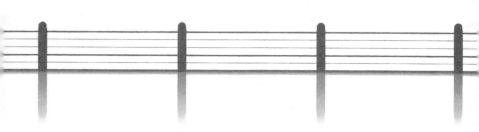

CHAPTER ELEVEN

LIVING GRATITUDE

On the whole, I do not find Christians, outside of the catacombs,
sufficiently sensible of conditions. Does anyone have the foggiest idea
what sort of power we so blithely invoke? Or, as I suspect, does no one
believe a word of it? The churches are children playing on the floor with
their chemistry sets, making up a batch of TNT to kill a Sunday morning.
It is madness to wear ladies' hats and straw hats and velvet hats to church;
we should all be wearing crash helmets! Ushers should issue life
preservers and signal flares; they should lash us to our pews.
For the sleeping god may wake someday and take offense,
or the waking god may draw us out to where we can never return.

Annie Dillard

Having considered gratitude's surprising blessings, as well as
some of the obstacles that can block its flow, how then to
develop a perpetual mindset of thankfulness? Is gratitude yet
another discipline to be mastered, a potential source of guilt,
another daily checkbox goal that grinds and binds us?

No.

After a chat with Chuck Colson one day, off I went to the dentist. Chuck and I had been talking about gratitude, and in passing
I mistakenly used the word "discipline" to describe it. Memo to
self: Never use an imprecise word with Chuck Colson.

"Gratitude is not a discipline," he growled, straightening his Prison Fellowship tie pin. "It is the response of the believer to the Spirit's work."

Soon after this I left Chuck's office, arrived at the dentist's, and settled into the chair. Dr. Funk injected Novocain in my front gum under my nose and in my jaw near my ear. Within a few minutes I couldn't smell or hear, but I was feeling no pain. Then the doctor called in a dental assistant, and the two of them commenced military operations in my mouth. To remove myself from the stress of the immediate situation, my brain and I entered a deep and reflective meditative state, pondering Chuck's words.

"He's quite right," we thought. Dr. Funk ground away. Tooth fragments flew through the air and settled in a fine dust on my soggy bib. "Gratitude is not a discipline. You can't fall into the trap of treating it like one. You can't resolve to be more grateful. Can't conjure it up by your own determined effort, or it will blow away in the first strong breeze. Can't go around telling yourself and others that we all must be grateful, we just really must, or you become a nag and no one invites you to Thanksgiving dinner.

"No, if grace is the gift of God, so too is the gratitude that grace creates."

Ah. My dental-chair epiphany was quite freeing, even after the Novocain wore off. But while a perpetually thankful heart is a gift, receiving it does depend on a discipline or two. Four, actually. There are four things that we can do to practice the presence of gratitude. When we do, we find that God further uncorks a flood of thankfulness.

The four things are quite simple. Any child can do them. So can most adults.

First, we remember.

Second, we forget.

Third, we look up to God.

Fourth, we look around to His people.

CHAPTER TWELVE

REMEMBER

It's a sign of mediocrity when you demonstrate gratitude
with moderation.

Italian actor Roberto Benigni

*R*emembering is an enormous theme throughout the Scriptures. It is potent; when we remember the right things, it will naturally trigger refreshing, empowering gratitude.

The English word for *remember* comes from Latin roots for *back* and *again*. It implies a mindful effort to recollect, to bring back again. The root word in Hebrew, *zakar*, has the same dynamism. It means to call to mind, celebrate, confess, extol, evoke, remind, report, record, preserve. All these are verbs. They denote action.

The point is, human beings don't tend to remember passively. We remember by a decision of the will, a purposeful action taken, a physical reminder set out where we can see it.

Certainly this is true in our national history. Memorials, statues, and monuments are placed in public places to remind us of sacrifices for our freedom, of individual acts of heroism that might otherwise be forgotten.

Just about every grand avenue and circle in Washington, DC, has its monument. They honor heroes of all kinds—statesmen, inventors, artists, thinkers. Most, however, are soldiers, known and unknown. Some are Civil War generals. These equestrian statues follow an unwritten code: if the statue's general is on his horse, with its four feet planted on the ground, the officer survived his war unscathed. If the horse has one leg raised, the general was wounded in battle. If the horse is rearing, two legs in the air, the hero was killed in battle. If the horse has all four feet off the ground, the general achieved sainthood.

Then there are the monuments at Arlington National Cemetery. I return often to my parents' graves there, just over the hill from the Pentagon, the Washington Monument piercing the sky, the white Capitol dome in the distance. My dad, an Army colonel, is in good company. Around him in the crew-cut grass are the markers of a twenty-year-old Marine who died during a foreign invasion, an old veteran of World War II and Korea, a colonel who survived Vietnam to die at home decades later . . . these ranks join the rows and rows and rows of white headstones, men and women who fought for freedom.

Up the hill is the eternal flame marking the grave of President Kennedy. It reminds me of other flames. Space shuttle Challenger explodes in 1986; its astronauts slip the surly bonds of earth. Now they lie here, commingled. Columbia disintegrates in flame above Texas in 2003, and its heroes, so close to home, fall still. I stare at the grave of Captain David Brown, Columbia astronaut. I remember our high school senior prom. The old photos in my scrapbook show Dave with his date, me with mine, standing in my parents' dining room, the four of us smiling, eager, young, looking ahead to we knew not what. David pursued his dreams, all the way to outer space. Now he rests in a narrow space at Arlington. Now, as President Bush put it, he and his fellow explorers "will always have an honored place in the memory of this country."[1]

In our corporate, national experience we expend effort to build monuments so that we might not forget what we must remember.

The same is true in our individual lives.

Our great friend Jerry is a lay minister and missionary. He is bold, sold out for Christ, and God is using him in venues Jerry never dreamed of. He leads a Bible study for television and print journalists. He unpacks the Scriptures with small groups of businessmen, politicians, professional athletes, and anyone else God leads him to. One of Jerry's outreaches involved helping a Moscow hospital for children with cancer. For a while he traveled back and forth to Russia fairly often.

One such trip was just before Jerry was to conduct the wedding ceremony for Ingram and Dave, friends whom he and his wife Holly had known for years and counseled during their engagement period.

The nuptial day arrived. Jerry had careened into town from Moscow the day before, but now here he was in place, upright, shaven, both shoes on, ready to perform the ceremony. He stood by the altar with Dave and his groomsmen. The church doors opened, the music swelled, the crowd of guests stood, and Ingram floated down the aisle, a vision in white. She arrived at the altar, where her old friend and mentor Jerry reached out tenderly to join her hand with that of her groom. Ingram looked down ... and there, in black ink, scrawled on Jerry's left hand, were the names "INGRAM" and "DAVE."

Jerry was wise. He knew he was exhausted, his brain scrambled from jet lag. He knew his flesh was weak, so to speak. So he took physical action to ensure that at the point of need, he would remember what he knew so well. He did not leave it to chance that at the key moment, he would wreck his friends' wedding by forgetting their names.

In our spiritual journeys, it's similar. Though we are always learning new things from Scripture, our primary challenge is simply to remember what we know. We must take action to ensure that we recall who God is and what He has said and done.

And that is precisely the point where Satan will assail us. He will lure us and lull us to do what comes naturally, and that is to forget God's truths. In the Garden of Eden, Satan didn't have to do a whole lot of heavy lifting. All he did was naggle at Eve . . . "Did God *really* say, 'You must not eat of any tree in the garden'?"

Of course, that wasn't what God had said, and Eve tried to correct the tempter. But she got it wrong. She told him, "We may eat fruit from the trees in the garden, but God did say, 'You must not eat fruit from the tree that is in the middle of the garden, and you must not touch it, or you will die.'"[2]

Eve misquoted God. He hadn't told them not to touch the fruit. And though that seems like a small error, it fit Satan's scheme, for he was luring her to forget God's goodness. In so doing, she also forgot His words. The Fall was not far behind.

Again, remembering will naturally elicit gratitude when we train our minds' recall on three main things. Each has parallels with the Old Testament people of God; these are also true for those who are part of His new covenant today.

First, We Remember That We Were Slaves

Slavery was a literal reality for the Old Testament people of Israel. Forced into servitude, they built cities, worked the fields, groaned and died under oppression. They yearned for deliverance.

It is difficult for many North Americans to identify with the horrors of actual slavery.

For African Americans whose ancestors came to the New World in chains, the reality is closer. Students of historical heroes like Harriet Tubman or William Wilberforce can hear the crack of the whip and see the separation of families, the cruelty of the overseer, the slave ship packed with its human cargo.

And students of the present know that slavery still exists. Researchers estimate that two million people around the world are enslaved by the international sex market.[3] They are mostly girls and boys who were stolen young; they live in dark corners, out of sight. Similarly hidden are the hundreds of thousands in the general slave labor market. Those who study the issue say that there are more slaves alive today than all the people stolen from Africa.[4]

So slavery's horrors still exist. But most of us can relate more with figurative, rather than actual, chains.

Two pictures hold this reality in my mind.

The first is of a Russian aristocrat. The second, an American crackhead.

At the end of the nineteenth century, the empire of Russia made up one sixth of the earth's land mass. As night fell on its western borders, the sun rose on its Pacific coast. Its ruler, Tsar Nicholas II, "Emperor and Autocrat of all the Russians," presided over a court studded with wealth and sophistication. Ballet, music, opera, drama, and literature flourished. Royals attended balls in nine-hundred-room marble palaces hung with gold and crystal chandeliers. Ladies flaunted diamond tiaras, shining pearls, sparkling sapphires, enormous rubies. After dancing until dawn with army officers in brilliant dress uniforms, they would nibble on lobster, pastries, and four kinds of caviar, sipping champagne and reclining on smooth silk sofas that rested on thick, velvet carpets.[5]

The autocracy could not sustain its opulent weight through war, political unrest, and the poverty of millions of Russian peasants. The sparkling, gilded court of the Tsar faded to black with the Russian Revolution. The royal family was taken into custody. And the imperial reign of the Romanovs met its end at about one o'clock in the morning of July 17, 1918, when the Bolsheviks executed Nicholas II, his wife, and five children.

But the lost grandeur of Tsarist Russia lives on in the prolific correspondence and journals of the Romanov family. And as I've read the ordinary yet poignant writings of that time, I came upon the anguished diary of Grand Duke Konstantin Konstantinovich. (Thankfully, he was known as KR.)

His grandfather was Tsar Nicholas I. Born in 1858, KR grew up in the competitive, extensive royal family. He was wealthy, athletic, artistically talented, handsome, multilingual, a musician of note, president of the Russian Academy of Sciences. He courted Princess Elisabeth of Saxe-Altenburg, married her in a lavish ceremony, and dwelt in imperial palaces. Intelligent, dutiful, accomplished, a great patriot, KR was one of the most admired men in his enormous country.

He was also one of the most miserable, a slave to secrets he confided only to his diaries.

> *November 1903.* [I have been called] "the best man in Russia." But I know what this "best man" is really like. How appalled all those people, who love and respect me, would be if they knew of my depravity! I am deeply dissatisfied with myself.[6]

> *24 November 1903.* I again feel a surge of renewed strength and am ready to do battle with my passions. It's always like this after I have fallen; but this time I think I have more determination than I did for instance 10 years ago . . .

> *15 December 1903.* Ten years ago . . . I began to struggle earnestly with my main vice, and did not sin for seven years, or more correctly, only sinned in my thoughts. In 1900, after my appointment as head of the military training institutions, I went astray. . . . Then it was better for two years, but in 1902 . . . I sinned a lot. Finally, this year, 1903, I have gone completely astray . . .

> *28 December 1903.* My life flows on happily. . . . I am loved, respected, appreciated, I am lucky and successful in everything that I do, but I lack the one essential thing: inner peace. I am completely possessed by my secret vice. . . . I am married, I have seven children and old age is not so far away. But I am just like a weather-vane . . .

> *20 January 1904.* As I was coming home, I ordered my coachman to turn right along the Moika channel. . . . I got out . . . and continued on foot past the bath-house. . . . I went in. I took a cubicle. . . . I have again become inexpressibly disgusting and revolting to myself. Will I never be free of this?

> *14 February 1904.* I am fasting, trying to attain the remission of my sins, or rather of my main, mortal sin, and hope that I will be successful . . .

19 April 1904. . . . I dream of going alone to the bath-house. . . .
I can picture the familiar attendants. . . . My predilection has
always been for simple men. . . . When passion speaks, the argu-
ments of conscience, virtue and reason are silenced.

21 May 1904. I was overwhelmed by sinful thoughts during
the committee meeting. . . . I walked up and down twice past the
bath-house doors; on the third time, I went in. And so, I have once
again sinned in the same way. My mood is absolutely foul.

26 July 1904. In the morning, the bath-house. And once again
I find myself, like a squirrel on a wheel, in exactly the same place.

I thought of the enslaved Russian aristocrat when I visited a
maximum security prison and met an inmate who was free.

As a young man, Kirk[7] had manufactured methamphetamines.
He ended up in prison, which saved his life. He got involved with
a Bible study program and received Jesus. He got clean. By the time
I met him, he was healthy, laughed easily, and was comfortable in
his own skin.

His life had been very different when he was "free."

Making street drugs wasn't hard. Kirk used ingredients like
over-the-counter cold medications, drain cleaner, battery acid,
antifreeze, and lantern fuel. The combinations of such compounds
created a chemical that had dramatic effects on the central nervous system. Kirk would maintain his highs by devouring his drugs,
going without food or sleep for days at a time. Over six feet tall,
he weighed about 125 pounds. He became violent, paranoid, heard
things that weren't there, and felt invisible insects crawling on his
flesh. He'd binge for days, crash, and begin the desperate cycle
again.

Before he went to prison, he was like a squirrel on a wheel.

Then, behind the razor wire, electronic doors, and bars—when
he was in a cage—Christ set him free.

Even if we're not hooked on drugs or struggling with a closet
vice, we are *all* slaves on a wheel until God sets us free. Whether
"small," heinous, respectable, or secret, sin enslaves. Think of what

Jesus told the religious leaders of His day. They were upstanding, reputable, and thought they were free agents. But Christ told them that if they were His disciples they would know the truth, and the truth would make them free.[8]

The men pulled their robes around them in horror. How dare He suggest such a thing? They sniffed, "*We* are Abraham's offspring, and have never yet been enslaved to anyone; how is it that You say, 'you shall become free'?"

Jesus told them that everyone who commits sin is a slave of sin. But when God sets people free, they are free indeed.[9]

Any addiction treatment program's success depends on people remembering where they came from. Gratitude follows. A friend, rescued from his active addiction to alcohol, keeps his glasses under his bed at night. In order to retrieve them, the first thing he must do each morning is get on his knees. There, he purposely remembers his slavery—and thanks God for his deliverance.

Again, maybe we weren't addicted to drugs or secret vice. But spiritually, we were all prisoners. Slaves to sin, headed to hell. Slaves to the fear of death, as Hebrews 2 says. And when we remember our former captivity, we overflow with gratitude for our freedom.

Second, We Remember Our Deliverance: At a Certain Point in History, God Rescued Us!

As any Sunday school kid knows, at a particular point in time, God put historic events in motion to rescue the Israelites from their slavery in Egypt. He raised up Moses to be their leader. He arranged a series of creative plagues for Pharaoh. He parted the Red Sea so the Israelites could pass through on dry ground—and then He drowned Egypt's pursuing army.

In the victory celebration that followed, Moses told the happy Israelites to bear in mind just how their deliverance occurred—

though at the time, they could not imagine ever forgetting God's great miracles.

"Remember this day in which you went out from Egypt from the house of slavery; for by a powerful hand the LORD brought you out from this place."[10]

We too have been rescued. There were no stopped-up seas for most of us, but our deliverance is no less dramatic. It doesn't matter if we know the exact day we were born again, the moment of our actual rescue from the slavery of sin and death, or not. The point is, we must remember God's intervention in our personal history, and the fact that He delivered us—not just from the sin-induced horrors of this life, but from hell in the next. *Hell.*

Third, We Remember Our Deliverer

The children of Israel didn't get out of Egypt and into the Promised Land by their own cleverness, courage, or power. At first, fresh from the miracles, they realized that full well, and they gratefully honored God.

But later, when they were well-off, they forgot who had delivered them.

Moses tried to warn them. "Remember how the Lord your God led you all the way," he said. "Revere *Him.*"

One can almost imagine the Israelites rolling their eyes. *There he goes again. Somebody give him a leg of lamb or something.*

> "Be careful that you do not forget the LORD your God," Moses droned on. "... Otherwise, when you eat and are satisfied, when you build fine houses and settle down and when ... your silver and gold increase and all you have is multiplied, then your heart will become proud and you will forget the LORD your God, who brought you out of Egypt, out of the land of slavery....
>
> "You may say to yourself, '*My* power and the strength of *my* hands have produced this wealth for me.' But remember the LORD your God, for it is he who gives you the ability to produce wealth...."[11]

But once the Hebrews became comfortable, they also became complacent. And they did forget.

In seasons of ease, it's easy to glide away from God. We become self-sufficient. We assume that our pleasant situations have something to do with us, that we are entitled to such blessings, that they in fact reflect our own good taste.

One modern-day Moses said as much. Sadly, things have not changed for the positive since he made these observations.

> We have grown in numbers, wealth, and power, as no other nation has ever grown. But we have forgotten God. We have forgotten the gracious hand which preserved us in peace and multiplied and enriched and strengthened us, and we have vainly imagined, in the deceitfulness of our hearts, that all these blessings were produced by some superior wisdom and virtue of our own. Intoxicated by unbroken success, we have become too self-sufficient to feel the necessity of redeeming and preserving grace, too proud to pray to the God that made us.

So wrote Abraham Lincoln in his 1863 Thanksgiving Proclamation.

We'd never do it consciously . . . but gradually, lulled, we forget our Deliverer and become callused with pride.

In this, we do well to meditate on the cross. Not the small, tasteful gold jewelry we might wear, but the big, bloody one on which Jesus died. The cross that delivered us from unending agony, flame, regret beyond imagining, dark terrors beyond comprehension. Christ's blood and His own torture saved us from our sin. Sometimes we're so familiar with the theology of the crucifixion that we become inured to its reality.

When we take communion, we do so in remembrance of Him. The Greek root of *eucharist* is *eucharistos*: grateful. When we remember the One who died in our place, we cannot help but bow down in wonder—and leap up with a bubbling spring of gratitude.

When Jesus Himself had given thanks at the Last Supper, He told His followers to take of His body and blood, "in remembrance of Me."[12]

"Cut yourself off from prying personal interest in your own spiritual symptoms," says Oswald Chambers, "and consider bare-spirited the tragedy of God, and instantly the energy of God will be in you. . . . We lose power if we do not concentrate on the right thing. The effect of the Cross is salvation, sanctification, healing, etc., but we are not to preach any of these, we are to preach Jesus Christ and Him crucified."[13]

Remember!

Psalm 107 tells us that thankfulness to God should constantly be on the lips of those whom He has saved. The psalm describes four kinds of people who have been delivered by God: wanderers, prisoners, rebels, and storm-tossed successes. Whether we fit just one or all of these descriptions, the psalm is a rich meditation for remembering our slavery, deliverance, and Deliverer. It begins with these words:

"Let the redeemed of the LORD say so, whom He has redeemed from the hand of the adversary."[14]

Many years ago, when I was young and wore a red bandana, I went to Young Life camp in the mountains of Colorado. The week ended with a "say-so," in which people could publicly give thanks to God for what He had done in their lives during camp. Many faltering adolescents, scared to death, bravely stood up in front of their peers and gave short testimonies about God's love and power.

These talks were not eloquent. Sometimes, as in my own case, they were almost incoherent. But they exercised an important principle: when we tell others how God has delivered us, we give thanks and honor to Him. We also plant a flag in the public record: *God did something here.* Others can take hope that He could do the same for them.

And later, when we are tempted to forget, we can look back at that small flag, fluttering in the breeze of memory, and remember that His deliverance was real.

Here's the say-so I couldn't have given as a teenager wearing a red bandana . . . for though I was a believer then, I wore chains that I was not freed from for many years.

CHAPTER THIRTEEN

OUT OF THE BLUE

It is not experience of life but experience of the Cross that makes
one a worthy hearer of confessions. The most experienced psychologist
or observer of human nature knows infinitely less of the human heart
than the simplest Christian who lives beneath the Cross of Jesus.
The greatest psychological insight, ability, and experience cannot grasp
this one thing: what sin is. Worldly wisdom knows what distress and
weakness and failure are, but it does not know the godlessness of men.
And so it also does not know that man is destroyed only by his sin and
can be healed only by forgiveness. Only the Christian knows this:
In the presence of a psychiatrist I can only be a sick man;
in the presence of a Christian brother, I can dare to be a sinner.

Dietrich Bonhoeffer, *Life Together*

E quindi uscimmo a riveder le stell.

And so we came forth, and once again beheld the stars.

Dante, *Inferno*, Canto 34

When I analyze my own rollicking experience of gratitude
these days—which is not nearly as fun as just living it—
there are several key catalysts.

One, as I said in chapter 3, is the reality of death, which reminds
me that every day is a gift.

A second, equally cheerful, is the reality of my rescue from the effects of clinical depression.

This is one of the things I remember when I reflect on God's deliverance in my own life.

Clinical depression bears a stigma among some Christians, who dismiss it as weakness, deficiency of faith, feelings that can be shaken off if one just shakes hard enough. Some believers seem to view any type of brokenness, insufficiency, problem, or handicap as a failure. They put forth a skewed version of the "victorious Christian life," a sham that postures glossy perfection and reflects airbrushed cultural values far more than the wounded realities of biblical victory.

One friend with a long history in religious publishing warned me, "Are you sure you want to write about depression? Might not the denial, repression, disingenuousness, and phony baloney of evangelicaldom rise up and call you a kook?"

I don't think so, if only for the reason that no one really says "kook" anymore.

The cause of any particular person's depression can't be analyzed like a chemical compound ... "Let's see, it's 16 percent because of your family background, 24 percent because of a chemical imbalance in your brain, 35 percent because of sin in your life, 7 percent because you're not getting enough natural light during the winter, and, uh, 13 percent because of your gene pool."

"But wait, that's only 96 percent!"

"Well, that's because you're depressed and not all there."

Perhaps all those elements are present, and more. Or less. We can't weigh out every gram of cause on our human scale. We do know that God is sovereign, and in the mysteries of His will He allows brokenness, weakness, and physical and emotional challenges. So it's no real surprise that Christians would reflect the same proportion of neurological imbalances as the general population ... that His compassion and care for human needs might be showcased.

Sometimes He heals miraculously. Sometimes He uses doctors and others as agents of healing. And sometimes He heals not in this life, but in the next.

But what He always does is use yielded human lives for His own glory. By His power, not ours. As Elisabeth Elliott has put it in a quote I love:

> It is not the level of our spirituality that we can depend on. It is God and nothing less than God, for the work is God's and the call is God's and everything is summoned by Him and to His purposes, the whole scene, the whole mess, the whole package—our bravery and our cowardice, our love and our selfishness, our strengths and our weakness. . . . [God uses] as the instruments of His peace a conglomeration of sinners who sometimes look like heroes and sometimes like villains, for "we are no better than pots of earthenware to contain this treasure [the revelation of the glory of God in the face of Jesus Christ], and this proves that such transcendent power does not come from us, but is God's alone." (2 Corinthians 4:7 NEB)[1]

My own pot cracked one crisp morning some years ago.

Having taken my children to the babysitter, I headed off to the dentist for a root canal. It was autumn, a season that pierces me with its sweet-sharp melancholy. It was also about a year after we had weathered a season of stress. We had adopted toddler twins. Having an instant family of three children under the age of four, two of whom I didn't know very well, taught me innumerable deep spiritual lessons. I just can't remember any of them.

We had also built a new house, sold an old one, and been the targets of a strange lawsuit that sputtered to a close after the judge in question committed suicide. While all that was going on, I had finished writing a new book, somehow meeting my deadline.

We had coped with the various pressures, seemingly without consequence, still doing all the things we were supposed to do, smiling big, not missing a beat. The picture of success. (The only clue that perhaps things weren't quite right was that every Sunday, after breakfast and multiple diapers and getting everybody ready in their cute little outfits and tidying our home so realtors could stroll through it while we were at church, I'd collapse on the clean kitchen floor. Weeping. Like clockwork. But then I'd stop and we'd all careen off to services.)

Now, months after the season of stress had eased, I arrived at the dentist's office. The first appointment of the day, I was ushered into the throne room. An assistant clipped a light-blue bib around my neck, settled me comfortably into the reclining dental chair and told me that Dr. Funk would be with me shortly. Muzak piped in pleasantly. The view out the nearby window was one of golden leaves and swaying trees.

I waited. Dr. Funk was taking a long time. I stared out the window, conscious of an odd, rising sense of panic. What if he injected too much Novocain and I had an adverse reaction? What if I died, right here? What if that tray, that row of dental instruments, that drill and swirling spit basin, were the last things I saw on this earth? What if this particular Muzak, which was at the moment cheerfully playing a rendition of Barry Manilow's "Mandy," was the last thing I ever heard this side of the grave? And after a decent interval, who would Lee marry?

Thoughts like this spun, skittered, and collided in my brain like bumper cars at an arcade. Sparks flew. My breath was short. I had never felt this way before.

Dr. Funk bustled into the room. "Sorry to keep you waiting—," he began, but stopped when he saw the look on my face.

I tried to settle down. I had waited weeks to get this appointment. These feelings were irrational. I could do this. No need to make a fuss.

Then the dam gave way. I could not do this. At that moment, I could not do one thing more.

I struggled up and out of the horizontal chair. Dr. Funk just looked at me, his eyebrows up.

"I'm sorry," I said, tears squirting out of both eyes. "I just can't do this."

He thought I meant the root canal. "That's all right," he said. "We, uh, often have that effect on people."

"It's not you," I said, my forgotten blue bib now soaked with tears and sticking to my shirt. "It's me. I cannot do this."

I remembered the bib, looked down, unclipped it and laid it on the reclino-chair. "I've got to go," I said. "I'll reschedule."

Barry Manilow was still singing. Dr. Funk followed as I fled the room. "Don't hurry!" he called after me.

I escaped the office and found my way to the car, sobbing. The events of the past year, in fact, the past in general, rushed by in my brain as if they were wreckage from the sudden burst of a dam. It wasn't the root canal. It wasn't stress. What was it? I had felt so sad, powerless, absolutely overwhelmed for months, or was it years? I couldn't remember.

I called Lee and cried into the phone. It will be so much easier for him after I'm gone, I thought, and he marries a nice blonde kindergarten teacher. No more complicated dark-haired woman messing up his workday.

Lee took control. "I'll go get the children," he said. "I'll make a doctor's appointment for you. You just wait for me at home."

That afternoon, we all piled into our powder-blue Sable station wagon, and everybody took Mommy to the Christian psychiatrist. They dropped me off, the three children all in their booster seats in the back, waving cheerfully good-bye as they went off to the mall and I went to consult with an expert as to just why I was falling apart.

The bad thing about such consultations is that the counselor or doctor is working off your interpretation of things. As I waited for the elevator, I imagined a number of ways the conversation could go. I could manipulate words and impressions; would he get at the truth? What was the truth about me? Or worse still, what if nothing was wrong and this was normal?

I went in, sat down, and told the doctor what had happened at the dentist's office, how I had hit the wall and now I was sliding straight down, my fingernails scrabbling in the cement, nothing to grab hold of. I told him how I'd always been a person with great heights and depths of feeling. I could look back as far as my childhood and see the pattern of undulation. But now it seemed that the depths were getting deeper, darker, longer. In fact, that's all there were. I couldn't remember any real heights lately. When I pulled back from my busy life and really thought about it, absolutely all I ever wanted to do was to go to sleep.

The doctor listened, nodding. I stared at him, troubled by a rising fear that he wouldn't be able to help, that living like this was my doom forever.

Those fears, at least, were relieved. "At your age ...," he began.

I looked down, suddenly terrified that I was still wearing the blue bib. "At your age, what you're describing is probably a chronic condition. I would think you'll need medication the rest of your life."

In the end, I walked out of the office with a prescription for an antidepressant and a date to see the doctor again in a month. The powder-blue station wagon swooped next to the curb, and the family picked Mommy up so we could head home and I could make a healthy, well-balanced dinner for everyone.

That day of the blue bib and the blue station wagon was the beginning of significant changes for me. The discussions with the doctor and the antidepressant laid the groundwork. Once I had adjusted to the medication (after falling asleep on my computer keyboard, in my closet, in business meetings, at the dinner table, and everywhere else), I found that its effects were like those of a pair of prescription glasses.

Before, I physically could not perceive the world clearly. Everything had become a dark blur. After, all the same problems and challenges and stresses were still there, but now I could see them accurately. Now I could do the daily work I needed to do, taking hold of challenges, wrestling with God on some things, repenting on others, and realizing with an unprecedented passion and freedom that the realities of God's grace were really for me. Before, I could believe they were true and efficacious for just about everybody but me.

Statistics show that as many as one in five Americans suffer from one sort of clinical depression or another. As I alluded earlier, the figures within the evangelical subculture are pretty much the same, though I've been told they are higher in Nashville. Part of me—the Marine within—feels like we should all just buck up, suck it up, get a grip. No need for medication.

But then I remember the dramatic difference an antidepressant made in my own brain chemistry. I would not hesitate to take an aspirin for a headache, or buy prescription lenses, or take medication for my thyroid if it was out of whack. Other people's experiences and outlooks may well be different. But for me, medication brought what was physically awry into proper balance and allowed me to perceive and appropriate the truths of Scripture in a deeper way than ever before.

I don't tend to dwell on all this. I'm not particularly interested in going back to my childhood or meditating on the emotional wounds—most of which were self-inflicted—of my past. I am relishing the present, and I feel like the blind man from Scripture: "All I know is this. Once I was blind—and now I can see!"

I still have dark days. These are part of the creative personality, and I would rather have their depths—and their corresponding peaks—than be tidy and even-keeled. But the depths are no longer overwhelming. Ominous waves still build, far out to sea, and rush in great roiling crests toward the shore. But now, rather than being crushed into the sand, battered, scraped, and not even sure which way is up, I can dive through them. I hold my breath as the cold water rushes over my head, popping up like a seal on the other side, eternally grateful to God for the fresh air in my lungs.

CHAPTER FOURTEEN

FORGET

Right now I'm having amnesia and déjà vu at the same time.
I think I've forgotten this before.

Steven Wright

When I remember the chains of depression that once bound me, I thank God for the joy of living free.

There is a corollary, opposite discipline that buttresses a thankful heart.

It is, of course, *forgetting*.

I find that forgetfulness is a curious thing. It comes to most of us quite naturally. But it is highly selective.

A friend took her kids to an afternoon movie and returned to the parking lot several hours later. She was quite proud that she remembered right where she'd parked her car. The only problem was, she'd left the key in the ignition—and the car was still running.

My neighbor Sandy told me about an acquaintance who left the grocery store, went on another errand, then realized she had forgotten her groceries. She went back and checked all the carts in front of the grocery. Her bags were not there. Someone must have taken them.

She marched to tell the store manager about the crime. "Could you describe your bags, ma'am?" he asked. "Paper or plastic?"

"They were plastic," she said confidently. "There were two." She went on to carefully list their contents.

"Oh," said the manager. "And might they be the two plastic bags that are hanging from your arm?"

The woman looked down. There they were, dangling from her left elbow.

Another friend—I'll call her Jan—was driving to Florida with her family one Easter break. She and her husband were taking turns driving. Their kids had on their pajamas; they were cozily snoozing. Jan's husband took the first shift, while she rested. At about midnight they traded, and he wearily crawled to the back of the van to get some sleep.

At one o'clock in the morning Jan was getting dangerously drowsy, so she stopped at an all-night place to get coffee. While she was paying for it, her husband came in the store, signaling to her that he was going to use the men's room.

Jan got back into the van and sipped her coffee. Sure enough, it perked her up. She was able to drive the next five hours without a problem. As the sun rose and the car was crossing the Florida border, the children yawned and stretched awake.

"Guys," said Jan, "can you wake Daddy up, please? We're going to stop for breakfast."

The oldest child unbuckled, turned, and leaned over into the back of the van.

"Mom?" he said. "Uh—Dad's not here."

Yes. Jan, who had forgotten to turn her cell phone on, had also forgotten her husband at the coffee stop, which was now three hundred miles away.

Most of us have stories like these. Forgetting seems to come quite naturally.

But why is it that we forget the wrong things? Why is it so easy to forget the spiritual truths we need to remember, like God's incredible love for us, His gracious work in our lives, His Word?

And conversely, why is it so easy to remember what we'd just as soon forget?

For example, I retain in my brain not just part but *all* of the lyrics to the theme songs to the most innocuous television shows of the 1960s and '70s. On a moment's notice, I could easily burst into all the stanzas of those great musical themes to *The Beverly Hillbillies, Gilligan's Island,* and, let's see, *Green Acres.*

And the sad fact is, if you're old enough to remember this golden period of television, you could sing right along with me.

> *Come and listen to the story 'bout a man named Jed,*
> *a poor mountaineer, barely kept his family fed;*
> *and then one day he was shootin' at some food*
> *and up through the ground came some bubblin' crude*
> *oil, that is. Texas tea . . .*

or

> *. . . if not for the courage of the fateful crew,*
> *the Minnow would be lost /*
> *. . . (echo) the Minnow would be lost.*

Now, if you don't happen to share this great cultural legacy, never mind. (The rest of you are humming uncontrollably now, and will not get those relentless, cheery tunes out of your brain for days.)

Why do I have total retention of Gilligan but not of Scripture? Why do many of us remember in great detail every embarrassing thing we've ever done? Why are some of us haunted by sins from our past, carrying their shame as if it was yesterday?

Just as gratitude will be unleashed to the measure that we remember three things—our slavery, our deliverance, and our Deliverer—so, too our spiritual vitality will flow as we forget three things.

First, We Forget Our Sins

This may seem to contradict the notion of remembering our slavery. But remembering that I was a slave and have been freed is different from recalling the particulars of specific sins, soaking in their shame, reliving their pain.

Now, certainly, we must remember our sins as we are able, in order to confess them! But having done so, we can let them go. This is basic, but we need to preach it to ourselves every day, for it is at the heart of the Gospel: If we confess our sins, He is faithful and just to forgive us our sins, and to cleanse us from all unrighteousness.[1]

A friend told me about his son's challenges with his car, and consequently with his auto insurance. It seemed that the son had incurred some reckless driving offenses that were an indelible part of his record. Accordingly, his insurance costs were approximately astronomical.

My friend went through a number of procedures; his son went to driving school; a judge was gracious. And the record was expunged.

It was too good to be true. Just for fun, my friend called the DMV, cited his son's entire name and social security number, and asked about citations on his record.

There was a long pause while the staff person checked the computer. She came back on the line. "Sir," she said, "we have no record of any offenses at all."

As my friend says, that's how forgiveness is. The fact that God forgets is like calling heaven and hearing, "There is no record of any offense." It's not that the offenses are still on the page, crossed out with heavy marker, and everyone can tell there was a big mess right there. Nor are they partially erased, but still visible. They are expunged. It is as if they never existed. As we said earlier, we are *justified*.

We need to take God at His word. The extent to which we dwell on and obsessively noodle on our own sins from the past—sins for which we have repented—shows the extent to which we really believe God.

If God does not forgive us fully, if He retains our sins and holds them over our heads to bedevil us, then Christ died in vain. We either believe Christianity whole hog or not at all. Let's not say that we believe the Gospel and then act as if we don't. The Gospel says that God forgives our sins.

But Satan would lure us to live in guilt and fear. He pulls us into the shadow boxes of memory, in which our worst sins replay on the walls of our minds, flickering with their shameful power . . . what if we just can't forget our sins?

We need to be very clear here, or we'll miss the liberating point. It's not as if forgiveness is real only if we experience some kind of holy amnesia. No. It is not up to us. It is up to God. And the Scriptures say that *God* forgets our sins.

> I will be their God, and they shall be my people . . . "for I will forgive their iniquity, and their sin I will remember no more."[2]
> I, even I, am he who blots out your transgressions, for my own sake, and remembers your sins no more.[3]
> "For I will be merciful to their iniquities, and I will remember their sins no more," says the Lord.[4]

The Gospel truth is that *God forgets our sins.* How His sovereign omniscience operates in this arena is a mystery. But if we cannot forget our wrongdoings, it seems to me that we have to act on faith. We didn't make this up. We couldn't: it's too good. When Satan stirs up memories to haunt us, we can choose to say, *I believe God. He says He remembers my sin no more. You have no power here. Go away, in Jesus' name.*

Second, We Forget Our Shame

This is closely linked with forgetting our sins. Sometimes, even if we have mentally let go of various specific sins, their residual shame still sticks. Shame can spur depression, dysfunction of every kind. But God gives us beautiful pictures throughout the Old Testament covenant story of His people and how their purity, once lost, will be restored.[5]

In Isaiah, God says,

Fear not, for you will not be put to shame; neither feel humiliated, for you will not be disgraced. But you will forget the shame of your youth, and the reproach of your widowhood you will remember no more.[6]

In the new covenant, the apostle Paul could have been a prime candidate for shame, hopelessly glugging first-century wine in order to forget the horrors of his past sins. He writes of not just his pharisaical pride, but the fact that he had presided over the harassment, imprisonment, torture, and murder of innocent human beings.

"I am the least of the apostles," he wrote to his friends in Corinth, "and do not even deserve to be called an apostle, for I persecuted the church of God."[7]

If Paul had chosen to harbor worldly regrets, they could have consumed him for the rest of his life. But, he said, "by the grace of God I am what I am, and His grace toward me did not prove vain."[8]

When I am tempted to despair in shame over past personal choices, I have found Paul's "Popeye prayer" enormously helpful. *But by the grace of God I am what I am.* God knows that I am dust. He has compassion on me. And His grace to me did not prove vain.

God's grace is stronger than our shame—most supremely, because it was defanged when Jesus died and rose again.

Hebrews 12 says that Jesus "endured the cross, scorning its shame." When He had completed His bloody work on our behalf, it was finished. He sat down at the right hand of the throne of God. Mission accomplished.

We can choose to believe this or not. But God's magnificent provision is more than ample: we can forget our slithering shame, for Jesus took it. He scorned it, beat it, broke it. We need not take it back.

This is supernatural. It is a miracle. It sets us free. We, who are forgiven much, can love much, overflowing with gratitude for our deliverance from sin and shame.

In spite of so great a deliverance, we have a tendency to hold on to one more thing we must release.

Third, We Forget Our Successes

This doesn't necessarily mean that we must forget how we won the sixth grade spelling bee, or the great projects we've completed, or viable accomplishments in various endeavors. We are to work and live with excellence as unto God, and He takes pleasure in our successes as they are offered to His glory.

But we should forget past successes if they have defined our identity or caused us to be complacent, smug, and self-congratulatory. We're not to fondle the past, dwelling on past glories. (Similarly, we must make sure that our stories of God's work and grace in our lives are not all old. If we can only point to instances of God's faithfulness from five years ago but have none from this week, then our connection with Christ is not very current.)

Again, Paul is a great model. In one of his letters he warns the Philippians against those who would put their confidence in human criteria and accomplishments.

If anyone else thinks he has reasons to put confidence in the flesh, I have more, he said, citing his power resume that many of his day would have coveted. He could have been a total prig. But his focus was not on his past.

> "But whatever was to my profit I now consider loss for the sake of Christ," he said. "... One thing I do: Forgetting what is behind and straining toward what is ahead, I press on toward the goal to win the prize for which God has called me heavenward in Christ Jesus."[9]

Paul's passion pulses from the pages of Scripture. Here was this triple-A personality type, driven to achieve, to excel, to accomplish great things. And after his conversion he easily could have drawn his identity from his celebrity status and his viable successes for

Christ . . . preaching to great crowds, penning great writings, persecuted for the Lord.

But Paul did not coast on yesterday's successes. He would be the first to tell us that no athlete wins his race with his head turned back to admire the laps he's already run. We win straining for the finish, *forgetting* what lies behind, eyes fixed on Christ alone.

As Paul ran his own race, he encountered torture, tedium, rejection, loneliness, shipwreck, snakebite, prison, pain. But God gave him all he needed—and his fountain of gratitude flowed.

"Rejoice!" he wrote from prison, even as his future held little promise but a Roman executioner's sword. "Rejoice!"

Again, Paul had learned that the secret of being content did not depend on what he had, but who he knew. He knew the Lord was near. He knew how to live so immersed in Him that gracious gratitude—and the corresponding peace of God—overwhelmed his earthly fears.

The only obstacles that keep us from the rich freedom that Paul enjoyed are our own cheap snares and doubts. We get lost in these when we look to ourselves, preoccupied by our sin, our shame, our success, as if it were all about us. But if we can forget these tangles and leave them behind, like Paul, we begin to see that God's love is bigger than we ever dared to dream.

CHAPTER FIFTEEN

LOOK UP:
THE GRANDEUR OF GOD

> If a person, at the same time that he receives remarkable kindness
> from God, has a sense of His infinite greatness, and that he is
> but nothing in comparison of Him, surely this will naturally raise his
> gratitude and praise the higher, for kindness to one so much inferior.
> Jonathan Edwards

The third habit of grateful people is that they, like Paul, *look up* and see God as God. When we look up to Him, we are first overwhelmed and awed, then full of gratitude that One so huge would deign to love ones so small.

The other day I caught a glimpse of this in a very ordinary way.

As I've mentioned, I love to paint old furniture and often do so quite badly. An old dresser had been living in our garage, and I wanted to spiff it up for Emily's room.

I should also mention that we store our giant dog's dry food in the garage. We buy it in fifty-five-pound bags from Costco.

One Saturday, I strode into the garage and commenced work on the dresser. Humming lightly, I pulled its drawers out, one by one, dusting them and preparing them for paint. Then I pulled out the big bottom drawer—and stopped short.

In it was a large, gray mound of fluffy stuff that looked like the lint you clean out of your dryer trap. Sprinkled around were lots

of dog chow pellets. For a moment I had no idea what I was looking at . . . until gradually, my sluggish brain put two and two
together and came up with four words.

Mouse nest. Mouse nest.

I screamed like a lady in a cartoon. The children came running.
Baby mice went running too, with bigger mice popping out of the
lint and herding them like the sheepdogs in *Babe.*

Eventually Lee arrived. Gender-based negotiations began. Lee
and Walker, being male, wanted to violently smoosh all the mice.
Meanwhile Emily, Haley, and I pled for their darling, little bright-
eyed lives. And we did not allow the male dog to have a vote.

So, since the feminine majority ruled, we had to deal with the
situation. (Actually, several mice lost their lives in the first moments
of the encounter, but that's not relevant to this story.)

The relevant part is this. We herded the mice into a big, deep
recycling bin. We carried the plastic bin to the woods near our
house, speaking gently to the mice as we walked. We told them that
we were going to set them free. We found a warm spot near tall
shade trees. Dappled sunlight filtered through the branches. A small
brook flowed nearby. Acorns and other nuts lay on the ground,
with lots of leaves and grass to make new nests.

Meanwhile the mice, terrified, ran into the corner of the box.
They piled on top of each other, heads down, telling themselves
that if they could not see us, then we could not see them. We gently tilted the bin on its side. They tried desperately to stay in the
box, their tiny paws scrabbling on the plastic.

Our intentions for the little mice were good. We knew more
than they did. We had provided for their every need. But they just
wanted to stay in the box. All they saw was that we were terrifying creatures much bigger than they, and they did not trust us.

Of course this is a faint, minuscule picture of our relationship
with God. But it gives a sense of the dynamic in our lives. To move
to the next level, to the new adventure, to the good place God has
for us, we must get out of the box where we feel safe. That means

looking up and seeing the huge and awesome God. Though that rightly causes fear, it can lead to trust as well. For though He is enormous, He is good. Holy fear can give us grateful hearts—even, as we'll see in chapter 16, in awful loss.

We live in a land that has largely lost a sense of holy reverence, let alone the transcendent. Most everything is assessed by the criterion, "How does it affect me?" In a supremely self-referential culture it's hard to conceive of anything that is so wholly Other.

But real Christianity requires that we look to God on His own terms. He is not tame, nor manageable. He's not a nice, comfortable McDeity or the Man Upstairs.

Far too often we trivialize the holy, perceiving God as an extension of ourselves. God is white, just like us. Or black, or Asian, or Hispanic, or whatever. He's from North America. Or not. God must be a Republican. Or a Democrat. Or most assuredly an Independent. We unconsciously assume He's whatever *we* are, just bigger, though He shares our little biases, quirks, and opinions.

No. God is huge. Mysterious. Multidimensional.

The prophet Isaiah saw a vision of God in about 740 BC. He wrote a clear historical record of his experience. He was not the same after it.

> In the year that King Uzziah died, I saw the Lord seated on a throne, high and exalted, and the train of his robe filled the temple. Above him were seraphs, each with six wings: With two wings they covered their faces, with two they covered their feet, and with two they were flying. And they were calling to one another:
>
> "Holy, holy, holy is the LORD Almighty; the whole earth is full of his glory."
>
> At the sound of their voices the doorposts and thresholds shook and the temple was filled with smoke.
>
> "Woe to me!" I cried. "I am ruined! For I am a man of unclean lips, and I live among a people of unclean lips, and my eyes have seen the King, the LORD Almighty."

Then one of the seraphs flew to me with a live coal in his hand, which he had taken with tongs from the altar. With it he touched my mouth and said, "See, this has touched your lips; your guilt is taken away and your sin atoned for."[1]

Before Saul of Tarsus knew God, he knew a lot about Him. He was zealous to kill Christians, since he knew God must share his bias against Jesus of Nazareth. Saul's religious credentials and his enormous ego were both quite impressive. "I had every reason to put confidence in the flesh," he said later. "As for legalistic righteousness, I was faultless!"[2]

But then came the real Jesus to Saul, on the road to Damascus.

The Light blinded Saul. He fell to the ground, eyes burning, small self forever humbled, changed for good.

He burns.

We cannot yet see God. For now, He hides, in light inaccessible. But He lavishes His presence upon our world in the clues of His creation. In this, even the smallest hint of God's immanence, even the tiniest shadow of the reflection of His glory, is cause for holy fear: awe mingled with thanks.

Recently I was driving at twilight down an ordinary road near our home. I looked up and saw the atmosphere had changed. Before me was a huge bank of purple clouds . . . an enormous mountain range in the sky. It threw off normal perspectives. Dwarfed by the vast towers in the heavens, the familiar way seemed to drop away. Swayed, I could barely hold the car on the road. The neighborhood I'd been living in all my life was microscopic, a world with too few dimensions in the frightening face of the infinite.

Just a flash; then the moment was gone.

A while ago I was walking briskly along the edge of the Pacific Ocean. It was a glorious day. My little beach was deserted except for occasional backward-kneed birds. Porpoises were playing in the sea, and I was overcome by the delight of it all. So I was singing hymns, quite boisterously and badly, as I strode along.

I came upon a big, shield-shaped pile of small, smooth stones nestled in the slope of the shore. It was low tide, so they were exposed. Then breaking waves rushed over them, and as the water receded, it chinkled clearly through the rocks with harmonic, high-pitched tones. I'd never heard anything like it: afternoon vespers sung by the stones. It startled me: as best as I can put it, the rocks were crying out to the glory of God.

The singing rocks reminded me of what Marty Jenco heard during his captivity in Lebanon. One April night his guards pulled him from his makeshift cell up a stairway onto the roof of his building. They took off his dirty blindfold. The moon was full. And even as Father Jenco felt the chill evening breeze coming off the Mediterranean, he knew his captors had brought him up to the roof to execute him.

He trembled, but not from fear. "I was absolutely expecting a bullet through my head," he said. But at "this roof-edge of my prison life, in the white luminance of moon and stars, with the smell and taste of the salt-sea-breeze, I knew love reigned invisibly."

He heard the traffic noises of Beirut far below, the distant murmurs of a tortured, fratricidal city. But all that was eclipsed: "I heard God's love singing to me and in me, modulating all the world's fantastic dissonances."

He gazed on the brilliant beauty of the moon, overwhelmed by the love of Jesus.

"I waited for my bullet, not thinking what a terrible sinner I was, not thinking I should be sorry for the bad things I did and the good things I failed to do. Rather I thought, 'Oh, how beautiful this is! How beautiful! Thank You, Lord Jesus! I love You, Lord Jesus! Thank You for everything!'"

Then one of Father Jenco's guards spoke softly, in broken English: "We know you have not seen a moon in months. Not even the sky. Because the moon is so beautiful this evening, we wanted you to see a moon."[3]

Years after Father Jenco's full moon in Lebanon, astronomers predicted that the Leonid meteor shower in November 2002 would be the most dramatic in centuries. At 4:30 in the morning of the appointed day, my alarm went off and I crept downstairs and outside onto our backyard deck. The plan was for me to check out the situation, and if it truly merited attention, I was to wake the rest of the family. I gulped a cup of hot coffee and tilted my neck all the way back so my face was parallel to the dark skies. Lovely night. No clouds. Stars. But no Leonids.

I thought lovingly of the sleep I was missing, rested my neck for a moment, and then craned heavenward again, searching, looking, waiting for something I'd never seen before.

Then, at the edge of my vision, came the first shocking stream of light, an utterly silent flame against the night that made me gasp out loud. Then another. And another. The hair rose on the back of my neck; this was alien. I ran, shouting, for my family.

> The world is charged with the grandeur of God.
> It will flame out, like shining from shook foil . . .[4]

In 2003, when Hurricane Isabel churned toward Washington, its foreign might spurred similar reactions. "Washington is a city preoccupied with power," a *Washington Post* journalist wrote just before the hurricane hit. "As such, its residents might profitably stop worrying about the White House and the Pentagon" and look offshore.

> As it clawed its way westward toward the United States . . . Isabel was a Category 5 hurricane—the most powerful force on earth. Its strongest steady winds blew at 160 mph—with gusts to 225— and its 60-mile-diameter eye was perfectly circular, with multiple inner walls. . . . Its symmetry was mesmerizing—a 300-mile-wide meteorological bomb with the delicate beauty of a flower.

National Oceanic and Atmospheric Administration researchers reported phenomena they had never seen before: planes flew into the storm and photographed "spokes" in the eye—streaks of cloud radiating from the center like spokes in a wagon wheel.

"We don't know yet what they are or what they mean," a spokesman said.

The *Post* reporter concluded:

> Hurricanes like Isabel . . . pack the power of several hydrogen bombs and the capricious nature of a cosmic cat toying with a mouse. . . . To experience a serious hurricane is to learn with terrifying comprehension precisely how small a mouse we are. And to appreciate, with an almost religious awe, the mind-reeling size of the cat.
>
> . . . When the Big One comes ashore, of course, it speaks with the voice of the Old Testament God. The one who gave the prophet Ezekiel the vision of the "big wheel."[5]

For his part, Ezekiel's report was filed in about 571 BC. "I looked," he said, "and I saw a windstorm coming out of the north—an immense cloud with flashing lightning and surrounded by brilliant light."

Ezekiel saw things he could not explain: wheels within wheels, full of eyes, moving, still, sparkling like ice, awesome. He heard the sound of wings, like the roar of rushing waters, like the voice of the Almighty, like the tumult of an army. . . . Then there came a voice, from a throne of sapphire, the figure like that of a man, full of fire, and brilliant light surrounded him. Utter radiance.

"This was the appearance of the likeness of the glory of the LORD," Ezekiel says. "When I saw it, I fell facedown."[6]

"I am ruined," Isaiah cried. The original Hebrew means "I am undone." Disintegrated. That is what happens when human beings get a glimpse of the utterly holy God. But because of His mercy, He does not leave people in pieces, facedown, their lips on fire. He heals, binds up, reintegrates. God puts us back together. Once broken, we can become truly whole.

And when we gain our reference point for all things from His cosmic grandeur and holiness—rather than from within ourselves—He will bear us up. Looking up to God's enormity can give us a place to rest and the capacity to give thanks, even in unspeakable tragedy.

CHAPTER SIXTEEN

GRIEVING, BUT STILL GIVING THANKS

I cannot understand how there's always the present,
and how quickly the present becomes the past.
notes jotted by Dean Meyers
as a teenager in 1965

Giving thanks is, at once, obedience to biblical commands, as well as
a response that springs out of actual—versus lip service—belief
in Bible truth about what I deserve (condemnation and all that goes
with it), and what God has given me (grace and all that goes with it).
Bob Meyers, reflecting on gratitude
after the sudden deaths of his wife and brother

Judy Meyers had a high tolerance for pain. Ever since her back surgery, she had suffered from terrible, stabbing distress in her sciatic nerve.

But it didn't slow her down. She hurt, coped, and maintained an immensely busy schedule, cheerfully keeping her home, work, and family of five sons and one husband in line like a five-foot-tall master sergeant.

Since she pushed herself to overcome pain every single day, she wasn't particularly soft on others when they were occasionally ill. So when Bob Meyers was suffering from stomach inflammation that kept him in bed for a few days, Judy's compassion was slightly unusual. She didn't tell him to buck up and get back to work. Instead, she brought him special meals, murmured how sorry she was that he was feeling so badly, and fluffed his pillows.

Bob and Judy had been married for almost twenty-seven years. They had five strong sons ranging in age from twelve to twenty-five, a spacious home and land in rural eastern Pennsylvania, a close extended family, a strong church, many friends . . . life was good in September of 2000.[1]

On the afternoon of Tuesday, September 26, Bob had been in bad shape over the weekend and into Monday, but now his pain was manageable. He was still in bed but planned to go to his office later. Judy came to his bedside before she went out to meet two of their kids at an after-school volleyball game.

"Thanks for taking such great care of me," Bob told her. "I really appreciate everything you've done over the last few days. I don't know what I'd do without you. . . . I'd sure make a terrible single man!"

Judy smiled. He was right. He wouldn't do very well alone.

But she didn't pick up on the opportunity to tease him. "You're welcome," she said. "I'm going to drop off some photos before I go over to the kids' school. I'll see you tonight. Love you!"

"Love you too," Bob said. The bedroom door closed behind Judy, and Bob heard her heels hit the wooden stairs. She grabbed her keys, crunched through fallen leaves on the driveway, and drove away.

About twenty minutes later, Judy was dead. And Bob *was* single. But he wasn't alone.

Driving the family minivan, Judy headed down Shelly Road near the Meyers' home. She approached a T-intersection at Route 63 and flicked her signal for a right turn as she drew near the stop sign.

At the same moment, two other vehicles were converging on the intersection.

A car approached from the right. Its driver saw Judy's minivan barreling straight toward him. It was not slowing down for the stop sign, even though her turn signal was on. He could see the woman inside quite clearly. Her hands gripped either side of the steering wheel. She was looking straight ahead, her eyes fixed. Maybe she was having some sort of medical emergency. She was just about to broadside him.

His heart jolting, the driver held his breath and gritted his teeth for the coming impact.

But before the van hit him, it hit a vehicle coming from the other direction: a 73,000 pound, tri-axle, fully-loaded dump truck. Its driver saw the minivan run the stop sign; now he was bearing down right on it at fifty-five miles per hour. He wrenched his wheel and hit his brakes, desperately trying to avoid it.

But the dump-truck's turn put the full force of its thirty-six tons directly into the driver's door of the minivan. The violence of the collision smashed the van, threw it twenty-five feet down the road, where it crashed into a guard rail, spun, flew another forty feet, and was hit again by a heavy pickup truck that arrived on the scene at just the wrong instant.

If Judy Meyers had come to that intersection two seconds earlier, or two seconds later, the story would be different. But she arrived at precisely the second that ensured the full impact of thousands of tons of force, splintered glass, and ruptured steel upon her petite frame. She died instantly.

Back at home, Bob had no way of knowing his once-whole world had shattered. He tied his shoes, grabbed his briefcase, and headed out the door. After the pain of the weekend, he was thankful to be feeling better.

A few miles away, Judy's sister heard sirens wailing. There must have been a terrible accident.

At the end of the workday, Bob picked up a voicemail from his son, Aaron, who was twenty-two.

"Dad," Aaron said on the recording, "Um, don't leave your office, okay? I'm coming down. Just wait 'til I get there."

Bob did some more paperwork while he waited. Aaron probably needed to use the copying machine.

But when his son came in the door, something was wrong. Aaron's face was blotchy. He had Jeff, a friend of Bob's, with him. They sat in two chairs facing Bob's desk. Jeff did the talking.

"Bob," he said, "what I have to tell you is a very hard thing, so you need to prepare yourself. There was a terrible accident today, and Judy was killed."

Bob felt the room spin. He stared at Jeff. "There's got to be a mistake," he thought. "It's got to be someone else. Someone else. Not Judy."

Jeff was still talking, giving bits of clinical information from the state police. Aaron sat in the chair across from Bob, weeping. Bob's brain couldn't catch up with the facts. Shock.

One thing he knew, though.

"I can't sit here and melt down," he thought, his eyes on Aaron as time wrenched out of joint and the milliseconds lumbered by. "I've got four other boys to tell. They've got to hear this from me, not someone else."

He grabbed Aaron and Jeff, and they raced down the stairs. By the time Bob got to his van, his brain was flashing like a movie marquee, just one word, over and over.

Widower.

Widower.

Widower.

This can't be, he thought distractedly. I'm forty-seven years old. Widowers are supposed to be in their eighties.

He pulled into his driveway. He called his oldest son on his cell phone. Uri and his wife were on a highway near their home in Florida. Bob told them to pull over so he could give them some hard news. And he listened helplessly, unable to hold and comfort them, as Uri and Stephanie sobbed into the phone. Then Bob called his son Mark, alone in his dorm room at college.

Meanwhile, the bleachers at the school volleyball game were full; the news of Judy's death spread through the crowd like an electrical current. But a friend managed to grab and sequester Steve and Mike Meyers before they heard. "You've got to go home," she told them forcefully. "Right now. No questions. Straight home."

Steve and Mike had no idea what was going on. But they saw that this was not a time to mess around. They piled into Steve's car and headed home.

By the time the boys got there, the house was full of friends from church. Bob ran out and met them in the driveway. He hugged them tight. And then he told them that their mom was dead.

What followed was awful, though full of comfort. Bob knew that Judy had put her hope for eternity in Christ alone. That meant she wasn't stuck in the mangled, bloody van. She was in the presence of God Himself. Free.

Bob was thankful her death had been quick. It was good that she had not suffered.

And as he thought about what lay ahead for the rest of the family, he realized he had a clear decision to make.

"What am I going to do now?" he thought in his typically analytical way. "Am I going to try to figure this out, question God, criticize, open myself up to bitterness? That's one route.

"Or am I going to trust Him?"

He pushed on the idea, seeing if it would hold, like a person testing the strength of a ladder's first rung. Was it strong enough to bear him? Could he bear it?

"You are trustworthy," he said slowly to God. "I don't know what You are doing or why. But I know You know. Whatever happens, I'm going to trust You to help us through."

The days that followed were a blur. Friends and family filled Bob's house. His brothers—Larry, Greg, and Dean—consoled and reminisced with him.

Bob and his brothers had been close growing up but had become even better friends as adults. Larry, the oldest, lived about twenty minutes away. Greg and his family lived next door to Bob. Dean was the only brother who'd moved farther from home; he lived and worked in the DC suburbs.

Dean had been the Meyers boy who fought in Vietnam. At twenty, he was an infantryman in the First Platoon of B Company, Fifth Battalion of the Seventh U.S. Cavalry. Living in the jungle, he and his platoon buddies endured leeches, vipers, and red ants. They developed ringworm and jungle rot. Years later, Dean wrote about a mission:

"To the rear I heard the simultaneous rapid fire of automatic weapons and the distinctive 'kakakaka' of the Russian AK–47 rifles. . . . I heard our platoon leader yelling into the radio transmitter . . . 'One killed and two wounded'—the words sounded unreal. The firing had lasted about twenty seconds. My dreams of home faded. I had nine months to go."[2]

A letter home in mid-summer 1969 described a "quiet" Fourth of July: "One of our platoons received some sniper fire, but no one was hurt."[3]

Months later, Dean volunteered to go on an army patrol near Phuoc Vinh, about fifty miles north of Saigon. Three North Vietnamese soldiers opened up on him with AK–47s. Dean fell in the jungle growth, "all twisted up in the tall grass like an animal that had been shot," according to the buddy who found him. He would have bled to death if not for fellow soldiers who bound his shattered upper arm, pled with him to hold on, and got him out of there.

Dean came back from Vietnam with a Purple Heart and other medals. He went through extensive, painful physical therapy, and many operations. Doctors told him he'd be permanently disabled, but Dean kept working his arm until he could play tennis, softball, and the piano again, as well as hike, canoe, and bike. He went to Penn State, became a civil engineer, and eventually joined a prestigious engineering firm in northern Virginia.

Dean's war experiences, and his faith, led him to live in an unusually intentional way. Vietnam had showed him life is short; Christianity showed him it was precious. So he purposed to spend his time and resources on what really mattered: people.

Sometimes that outlook was countercultural. In the affluent, acquisitive DC area, he chose to live frugally. His TV was old; his stereo system still had a turntable. He packed his lunch each day for work. He used the money he saved to sponsor needy children in developing nations. He helped neighbors, traveled to Pennsylvania about once a month to do chores for his elderly parents and visit his brothers, gave to charities for the blind, conservation groups, ministries. He was often late to meals because he just would not cut conversations short. If someone needed to talk with Dean, he was available.

Dean arrived at Bob's home the day after Judy's accident, and in his low-key way, supported Bob and the boys however he could. He didn't mouth platitudes from a distance. He plowed through the loss right with them. He had loved Judy and mourned her sincerely.

Nearly 1,200 people came to Judy's viewing and funeral. Earlier in the day, before everyone else arrived, Bob and his boys had looked down at Judy's body in the coffin. They had dreaded this moment, but she had been mended and simply looked quite still. There was a silence. Then Uri, the oldest son, spoke. "It's like she's a house," he said. "And nobody's home!"

It was an odd way to put it, but they all knew what he meant. Judy was just plain gone. Only a shell was left. Bob felt an incredible wave of gratitude for her, for their marriage, for their years together as young lovers, new parents, confidantes, friends, intimate allies growing together over time like two close-planted trees whose roots become indistinguishable from one another.

He looked down the long aisle of the years ahead . . . birthdays, graduations, weddings, grandchildren, life's milestones . . . they would all come, without Judy. He didn't know what to do without her. But he did know they couldn't orient their lives backward, anchoring everything in her absence. She would want them to move forward.

Bob looked at his boys as they stood together around the casket. Judy wasn't there. She was with Christ. "You know what?" Bob said to his sons. "We can do this. God can give us the strength to do this."

They all nodded. It was like a pact.

Two years went by. During that time, Steven graduated from high school. With friends' help, Bob threw a huge party, just as Judy would have done. They missed her enormously, but they didn't live in the past. Fall came again, and golden leaves fell from the big trees next to Bob's driveway. Bob developed a relationship with a friend from church, Lori, who had known and loved Judy as well.

Meanwhile, 160 miles away, in the suburbs of Washington, DC, an unknown sniper was creating a dark wave of terror, randomly shooting people as they went about their daily business. Six had died, and two were wounded. The killer was still at large.

The sniper shootings were all over the news in rural Pennsylvania. Bob shook his head. It was so horrible and random and evil. He grieved for the families of the victims. He knew how awful it was to experience sudden, shattering loss. But he didn't stop to worry about Dean. Dean was just one of millions of people in the DC area.

On October 9, 2002, Bob was watching the eleven o'clock news. There were pictures of a northern Virginia gas station, a nondescript car with its gas tank door still open, yellow police tape strung around the pumps and fluttering in the rainy wind.

"Oh, no," Bob thought. "The sniper got somebody else."

Indeed he had.

Dean Meyers had worked late on the night of October 9, leaving his office a little after 8:00 p.m. He stopped to get gas before his drive home.

Dean pulled into a Sunoco station near his office. He took his ATM card from his wallet and flipped open the gas tank door. As he stood next to his car, clearly visible from a distance in the station's bright lights, there was the muffed crack of a gunshot. It was a copper-jacketed .223 bullet from a rifle similar to the one Dean had carried in Vietnam. Traveling at a velocity of 3,000 feet per second, it pierced his skull just below his left ear, tore through his fine brain, and shattered into fourteen pieces.[4]

Dean died instantly. He fell to the ground, his foot against his car tire and his head on the curb of the pump island.

At five o'clock the next morning, Bob Meyers woke to the ringing of his doorbell. He stumbled downstairs to find his nephew, Jason, and his wife, Christine. "We have something to tell you," said Jason.

Bob went to wake up Aaron, and within a few minutes the two of them were seated at the big dining-room table, groggily wondering just what was going on. Bob assumed that his mom or dad had passed on—though he wondered why Jason was here and not one of his brothers.

Jason gave it to them straight. "The DC sniper got Dean," he said. "He's dead."

Bob felt the same wave of absolute disbelief that had rolled over him when Judy died. "There's got to be some mistake," he thought. "Not Dean!"

Within an hour, Bob and other family members were at his brother Greg's house, trying to figure out what to do next. "Did Dean have a cemetery plot?" someone asked. No one knew. But even if he did, they decided together, there was no way they were going to bury him in the DC area, not with the sniper still loose. They talked about plans, logistics, and how they would respond to Dean's murder.

Bob kept thinking about the day of Judy's passing. It was as if her death had been a dress rehearsal for Dean's—with an important distinction. Judy's death was an accident. Dean's killing was intentional. Someone had looked down his rifle sights, centered Dean in the crosshairs, and pulled the trigger. Someone had made an evil choice.

But that crime did not strip Bob and his family of their own ability to choose. How would they respond? With bitterness, blame, regret? Or would they trust God? Together, they thought it through. Later, Bob would give a summary of their decisions to every journalist, reporter, and interviewer with whom he spoke. As Bob would tell Larry King, "We certainly would prefer that the circumstance wouldn't be the way it is. But on the other hand, if we're having to face the situation, we're going to do it by trusting God rather than questioning Him, and that helps us."[5]

The most pressing issue of the morning after Dean's murder, though, was the question of how to tell their father. Harold Meyers was eighty-three. His wife, Dean's mother, suffered from dementia and was pleasantly oblivious to much of what was going on. They hoped that the awful news wouldn't wound her in the same way. But Harold would need to be told soon, before he heard about his son's death on radio or television.

Larry, Greg, and Bob Meyers drove to the senior Meyers's stucco Cape Cod–style house with its peaceful views of rolling Pennsylvania hills. They stood on the porch, took a collective breath, and walked into their parents' cozy kitchen.

Their father had heard them coming. He met them just inside the door and clapped them on the shoulders, his face split by a huge grin. "What is this?" he asked. "Is it my birthday or something? What's going on? A Thursday morning and you guys are here to see me? Come on in!"

They made him sit down in the living room. Bob and Greg each clasped one of their dad's hands as Larry told him what had happened to Dean. The brothers bowed their heads as their father sobbed, his shoulders shaking in his plaid flannel shirt.

"Not Dean!" he cried over and over. "Dean wouldn't hurt a fly!"

Over the next twelve days, three more people were murdered and another severely wounded. Then police arrested two drifters named John Allen Muhammed and Lee Boyd Malvo. Malvo boasted to investigators that Dean's murder was an excellent hit, a devastating head shot that pulled police away from the sites of the previous shootings and thinned their resources.[6]

Dean had survived Vietnam but not a trip to the gas station. Two inches to the right, and the bullet would have missed.

Where was God when Malvo and Muhammed took aim? What was He thinking when Judy approached her fatal intersection? What are His intentions in the midst of crimes and accidents? Are there any accidents?

"Judy's death was a cataclysmic event, but it stopped short of what happened with Dean," Bob says. "The idea is the same, though. In both cases, God could have changed it, but He didn't. God didn't initiate evil intent in the human being who killed Dean. Nor did He intervene. Instead of trying to figure it all out, even though it doesn't make a lick of sense to me, I have to rest in the fact that God knows what He's doing."

The trap, Bob says, is to try to figure out tragedy from an inherently limited, *human* point of view. It becomes a control issue: if we can just figure out *why* this happened, then we'll be able to manage it.

"There's no way I could reconcile Judy or Dean's death into a human frame of reference," Bob says. "Trusting God springs from buying into Bible truth, which makes clear that God is God and I am nothing. I have to release my tendency to want to protect myself through controlling everything I can possibly control, in favor of trusting God implicitly in all things.

"Isaiah 55 says 'As the heavens are higher than the earth, so are my ways higher than your ways and my thoughts than your thoughts.'[7]

"The comparison between God's ways and mine, of His thoughts and mine, is the difference between heaven and earth. That's not a two-inch gap. It's *huge*. And I have to back off. I either believe that God is good and He is in control, or I don't. That's not easy ... but it's simple."

On the Sunday before Thanksgiving 2002, Bob and his sons and friends gathered for an early Thanksgiving dinner. It had been six weeks since Dean's death. Harold and Rose were there, though by the following Easter Rose would be dead and buried next to Dean. A DC journalist and a photographer joined the family for the feast. They recorded their visit with the Meyers clan in a front page story for the Thanksgiving Day edition of the *Washington Post*. The headline?

"Grieving, But Still Giving Thanks."

CHAPTER SEVENTEEN

LOOK AROUND:
CIRCLE OF FRIENDS

He who dares the most, shall win the most; and if rough be thy path
of love, tread it boldly, still loving thy neighbors through thick and thin.

Charles Haddon Spurgeon

Oh, the comfort, the inexpressible comfort of feeling safe with a person;
having neither to weigh thoughts nor to measure words
but to pour them all out, just as it is, chaff and grain together, knowing
that a faithful hand will take and sift them, keeping what is worth keeping,
and then, with the breath of kindness, blow the rest away.

Dinah Mulock Craik, 1859

In his deep, dark trench of tragedy, Bob Meyers chose to look up. His awed perception of God's enormity did not give him answers to the awful things that had happened. But his choice to see God as God gave him a place to rest in the midst of the unexplainable. Looking up also gave the Meyers family the means to give thanks in calamity. This demonstrated God's power for the nearly two million readers of the *Washington Post* on Thanksgiving 2002 far more clearly than would a thousand eloquent sermons.

If *remembering*, *forgetting*, and *looking up* are three disciplines of a habitually grateful heart, there is at least one more. It is to *look around*.

By this I mean that we make the conscious choice not to isolate ourselves, but to look around and connect in the fellowship of friends. The community of believers is an antidote to the discontent, depression, and despair that can come so easily when we sit alone. It can refresh us and pull us toward thanks and praise.

The fact is, Satan stalks us. If he cannot snatch our souls for eternity, then he tries to render our lives impotent for Christ on earth. He incites ungratefulness. He stokes dark feelings. And one of his most effective strategies to do so is to isolate us and keep us focused downward and inward. That's why looking up to God, tilting our faces toward heaven, choosing to believe His promises, is such a powerful weapon. So too is looking to our brothers and sisters in Him.

For when God pulls us into a vertical relationship with Himself, He also draws us into a horizontal relationship with other believers. No follower of Christ is alone. We are filled with the Spirit of God, and Christ is with us. We are also part of a camaraderie that the Bible calls the Body of Christ: people knit together forever, not by natural affinity or hobbies or political affiliation or socioeconomic similarity, but by God Himself. It's astonishing: the flawed and warty fellow believers like us with whom we worship in our local church are in fact mighty warriors, part of an eternal, invincible army with blood-red banners flying, ineffably stronger than the dark gates of hell, or anywhere on earth.

It is intriguing—to me, at least—that while I was writing this chapter, a cloud of fear and despair drifted over Northern Virginia and then chose to settle, invisibly, right on my house, specifically on my desk. My faithful dog, lying on the couch a few yards away, was not affected, but I felt pulled down by such a dark, strong tide of hopelessness. Nothing like writing a book about gratitude and then suddenly be walled from feeling it.

As I've mentioned, my "normal" personality tends toward depression, and writing is a vocation that lends itself quite readily to this disorder. So I expect ebbs and flows within my days. But this odd sensation was different and stronger than usual, as if a self-contained prison cell had dropped from the sky and landed precisely around my desk chair, hemming me in. Then the sides closed from the top down, like the black armored plating securing the Batmobile, or like those heavy hurricane shutters in Florida that descend over the windows and seal you in.

I was also in the midst of planning talks for a retreat, and preparing to teach a Bible study the next morning. This sense of being shuttered in, alone, depressed—was it spiritual warfare to distract and derail me as I prepared to share the Gospel?

Perhaps.

I prayed. I also "looked around," so to speak, by emailing my husband and four friends. I told them about this intense sense of oppression and asked if they would pray for me. Even though I felt dark and alone, I knew I was not.

Several interesting things happened. First, Lee and the other friends prayed. I kept trying to work; as the hours passed I began to feel a tiny bit better.

Second, my doorbell rang. I had sent our friend John Eddie an email asking for prayer, and now here he was on the front porch, bearing a cup of Starbucks double-shot mocha with whipped cream on top. He handed it to me and left in a cloud of kind goodwill.

I was gratefully downing the coffee when the doorbell rang again.

I went to the door, thinking that maybe John was back with another installment of grace, like a bagel or something. But it was our friend Holly, who never stops by during work hours. I had not sent Holly an email asking for prayer. But here she was on my doorstep.

"What are you doing here today, of all days?" I asked her.

"Hey," Holly said in her Southern way. "I was out, and then God gave me this sense that I should come over and pray with you."

"But I didn't send you an email!" I sputtered. "How did you know to come?"

"I guess God IM'd me," said Holly.

She came in, we prayed together, and then she left.

I felt better indeed. The dark and unusual cell-cloud was gone. And I was tempted to spend the rest of the afternoon peeking out the front door, waiting to see who would drop in next.

Now, this was wonderful, though I don't expect that every time I feel oppressed that people will swing by with coffee and prayers. But I do know that the principle here is important. Satan wants me to feel dark and alone. And the best actions I can take at times like that are to look up to God, and look around to His people . . . not just down at myself, or I will swirl deeper and deeper into glum paralysis. Those actions of looking up and around may sound simplistic, but for me they're strategic.

My own experience pales next to others I've heard.

Our pastor, John, was in Cuba recently. Though it's an island, the believers there know they are not isolated from the broader church around the world, and certainly not from one another. A Cuban believer told John how her baby son had been quite weak and ill. The monthly milk ration was used up. The family had no money. They had no hope of meeting their son's needs themselves. They prayed for God to provide.

A little while later there was a knock on the door of their small home. Two fellow believers stood there. One held a bottle of milk, wrapped in some old cloths to keep it cool. "God told us to bring you some milk," she explained.

Years ago I heard a similar supernatural story when I interviewed a Russian poet named Irina Ratushinskaya.

Irina is a believer who was convicted in 1984 by the Soviet state for the crime of "anti-Soviet agitation," which in her case consisted of writing poetry that celebrated human dignity and faith in God. She was sentenced to seven years hard labor in the gulag. Her case drew the international attention of human rights groups, writers, and Christians in the West, and in 1986, two days before Mikhail Gorbachev's Reykjavik summit with President Reagan, Irina was released.

She wrote about an unexplainable experience that happened repeatedly during her imprisonment. Tortured by cold, held in isolation in a cruel Soviet prison cell, she would nonetheless *know* that she was not alone.

> *Believe me, it was often thus:*
> *In solitary cells, on winter nights*
> *A sudden sense of joy and warmth*
> *And a resounding note of love.*
> *And then, unsleeping, I would know*
> *A-huddle by an icy wall:*
> *Someone is thinking of me now,*
> *Petitioning the Lord for me.*
> *My dear ones, thank you all*
> *Who did not falter, who believed in us!*
> *In the most fearful prison hour*
> *We probably would not have passed*
> *Through everything—from end to end,*
> *Our heads held high, unbowed—*
> *Without your valiant hearts*
> *To light our path.*[1]

(I interviewed Irina and her husband, Igor, in 1989—not in the old Soviet Union, nor in Washington, DC, but in the incongruous setting of a hotel in Costa Rica. I remember sitting with them at an outdoor table under a striped umbrella. Warm winds ruffled the palm trees as I listened to their stories of the gulag and cold communist oppression as they chain-smoked unfiltered cigarettes. At one point Irina broke from her narrative and stared moodily at the rectangular blue waters of the hotel pool. "Ah," she said in her heavy Russian accent, taking a long drag on her cigarette. "Swimming pool . . . eet eez prison for water.")

Looking to other believers is like seeing concentric circles from a pebble dropped in a pond. We are part of a small circle of friends . . . and a larger local church fellowship . . . and a regional company of believers . . . and the worldwide Body of Christ. Every believer is part of the "church universal," the company of Christians around the world with whom we are one, in spite of differences in language, culture, and worship styles.

I love to taste the sweetness of that fellowship abroad. It's just an hors d'oeuvre, so to speak, of the great feast to come in heaven, where no cell-clouds exist, nor separation, nor isolation.

Recently I went to Romania to speak at a little retreat on the theme, appropriately, "Taste and see that the Lord is good." This trip was through a ministry called Romanian Christian Enterprises, which helps widows, orphans, and the poor.[2]

I had first visited Romania in 1990. It was just a few months after the uprising that had overthrown the nation's communist tyrant, Nicholae Ceaucescu. At the time I was writing a book with Chuck Colson called *The Body*, which included the story of how believers had sparked that peaceful revolution. I interviewed many who had been part of the crowds that swelled Romania's city squares, holding candles aloft in the night, praying the Lord's Prayer, standing against repression.

In addition to my writer/interviewer role during that 1990 trip, I was also part of a team of Americans teaching in Romanian churches.

We traveled part of the time with Dr. Carl F. H. Henry, founding editor of *Christianity Today*, author of many brilliant books, and one of America's most influential evangelical theologians. Dr. Henry is now in heaven, but back then he wore an old raincoat and a black wool beret, and made himself quite at home in simple settings, gamely eating tuna fish out of cans he carried in his briefcase.

One night heavy rains soaked our shoes and socks. I remember Dr. Henry, courtly gentleman and esteemed scholar, sitting on the bare floor of a drab Romanian apartment, his sock in one hand and a hair dryer in the other. The hairdryer was not happy with the haphazard electrical current and was on half-speed at best, pitifully puffing on the wet sock with little effect.

At the time conservative Baptist Romanian women did not wear jewelry or makeup, and covered their heads in church. In deference to our hosts, the women on our team earnestly followed these guidelines—though we learned just how dependent some of us had been on cosmetic enhancement. Our bare faces were the shade of bottom-dwelling fish underbellies, our lips pale, our limp hair swaddled in scarves. We smelled of wet socks, looked like the undead, and were scaring the locals.

Dr. Henry perused us with his keen eye. He cleared his throat. We waited expectantly for some theological insight, knowing he no doubt appreciated our cultural sensitivity and would commend us for our Pauline faithfulness in seeking to be all things to all people. "You know," he intoned in his trademark quavery voice, "you girls look a *lot* better with makeup."

Well, as I said, I returned to Romania recently. The world had continued to change, and I had too. (Also, fortunately, I was able to wear makeup on this trip.) Our then eleven-year-old daughter, Emily, was with me. In addition to the retreat, we were seeing the work of Romanian Christian Enterprises. I wanted Emily to glimpse that the world is much bigger than our comfy corner of it and that we are part of a fellowship much greater than just in the U.S. We were traveling with nine other American women and girls.

We met Dinu, who welcomed us into his rural home. He had no kitchen, bathroom, or running water. His floors were packed dirt that had been brushed to a shine and actually painted in anticipation of our visit. Dinu's wife had gambled away their savings; they lost their former home. Then, pregnant with another man's child, she had ended up in prison. The baby girl was born and put in a state orphanage.

When Dinu discovered the baby's existence, he took her in, even though she was not his. He and his older children began going to church. They received Christ and were baptized. RCE helped them with a small loan; Dinu planted carrots, lettuce, and cabbage. His crops came in. He paid back the loan and made a profit.

Now he escorted us over carefully placed wooden planks through the barnyard mud and to a greenhouse covered with heavy plastic. We peeked inside—and there were thousands of young watermelon plants, their roots going deep in the tended earth, giving off a rich smell full of promise and hope.

We traveled later to a remote village populated almost entirely by elderly residents. The young people moved away to find work elsewhere. The school closed. And now the buses don't even run to Minsk.

But believers have not forgotten the little town. Every other Wednesday, a doctor and her nurse come to Minsk. A white flag with a red cross flies from the old church steeple to announce their presence, and the elderly people gather. Dr. Daria, herself on crutches, stays all day and into the evening, until each one has been seen and treated.

We watched one wrinkled widow making her way up the hill in a cold rain, leaning heavily on two stout sticks, her back bent almost double by osteoporosis, her head at waist level. A crowd of about twenty-five other elderly women parted to let her pass so she could be first to see the doctor. Meanwhile Emily motioned to the other ladies, asking if she could take their picture. They giggled like schoolgirls, straightened their babushkas and long aprons, and grinned toothlessly for the camera.

On another day, in another town, we met a smiling middle-aged woman named Florica. In the volatile days of Romania's revolution in 1989, her husband, a factory worker, was forced by the communists to defend their town's city hall. In the confusion he was shot and killed by government troops.

Florica had no means of support and two children to feed. In the months and years that followed her husband's death, her church family helped her. There wasn't much to eat, and they were cold in the winter, but they had just enough. Florica knew that God and His people were with her even if her husband was not.

So she did what was humanly impossible. She went to RCE's in-country adoption agency, *Speranta Copiilor*. "I don't have much," she said. "But God has blessed me. I am rich in love. I have enough love to share with children who have none."

Florica adopted two abandoned, throwaway children who had been in Romania's notorious orphanages. Their adjustment was difficult. But Angie and Vasile took root and grew like the green plants in Florica's garden. Today they are in high school, play mandolin in their church's youth orchestra, and are full of promise.

RCE gave Florica a pig. Like everything else in Florica's humble home, the pig grew and thrived. It had piglets. The family made it through another long, cold winter. Spring arrived, and Florica looked around. One of her neighbors, a widow, was having a tough time. Florica took her a piglet. "God has blessed me so much," she said. "Take this pig . . . in Jesus' name!"

One evening when we were in another town, our little group of Americans was invited to speak at a church meeting. Through our translator, each of us gave a snapshot of our experiences in Romania. Our friend Laura surprised us as she told how the trip had affected her.

"I want to tell you how I've tasted and seen that God is good," she said. "During our time here I have tasted the sweetness of your love for one another, and for us. And I've tasted the tartness of how you are bursting with energy to help one another through very hard things.

"I've had some hard times too. Two years ago my sister died. She was a believer. But she took her own life. I miss her terribly."

As these short, painful sentences were translated, the Romanian women had tears in their eyes.

"But on this trip," Laura continued bravely, "I've seen that I could *stay* in that valley of grief and anger and sadness. God has shown me that there's a danger of defining ourselves by tragedy. It can become our identity. On this trip, God has given me the nudge I needed. Now I can look around and taste God's goodness. Now I think I can move on. Now I can try to help others, like you do, with such sweetness."

The day before our departure from Romania, we were hosted at a home for orphans called Darius House. It is bright, airy, its yard full of flowers and its barn full of farm animals and a gentle golden retriever named Elsa. The children who live there were rescued from stark orphanages. Several are autistic, some have attachment disorders, others have cerebral palsy, muscular dystrophy and other problems. All are dearly loved at Darius House, from which some will be adopted by loving families.

One of the kids, Ionica, came from a state psychiatric orphanage where children were sedated and tied in their cots. When he came to Darius House at age five, he had not been toilet trained. He had never seen a fork or spoon. He could not speak. The government deemed him "irrecoverable."

Within a year of arriving at Darius House, Ionica was recovering. One summer night he was sitting with his friends by a bonfire at a camp. He watched the sparks from the campfire float upwards into the dark.

"Do they fly up from the fire to become stars in the sky?" he asked.

From no speech to poetry, within a year.

Now, during our visit, Ionica and his fellow poets sat in a big circle on the carpet and sang songs in English for us.

You're my friend,
1–2–3,
all my friends are here with me!

For the second verse, two of the autistic children struggled to their feet and danced awkwardly together . . . and for the third, they pulled one of their teachers into the circle before collapsing into a laughing heap on the floor.

Later, at lunchtime, I found that I was feeling ill. So I went to one of the children's rooms, just off the main area where lunch was being served, and closed the door. The head of little Otilia's narrow bed was near an open window. Outside, the children, including my Emily, were playing with the white lamb that lives at Darius House. It was running in big circles around the house; periodically I could hear its little hooves thundering past on the green grass outside the window.

I lay on Otilia's bed, my eyes shut, my head spinning with fever. I thought about Otilia with her shining brown pigtails. Once abandoned, now she was going to a school for gifted children. I tried to imagine what it was like to lie in this little bed every night, longing to be adopted. What was it like to be seven years old, to have cerebral palsy but no mom or dad, yet to have this family of friends, 1–2–3, at Darius House?

My mind spun in a dizzy merry-go-round. I heard bursts of laughter out in the main room, children singing, then baaing as the lamb went galloping by outside. There were conversations in English, Romanian, and a mixture of the two. And then I heard the sound of my own daughter—herself adopted—laughing as she helped a handicapped child to catch the lamb and hold him fast. We had both come a long way to be part of this circle of friends . . . and I was grateful.

PART FOUR

EVERYDAY GRATITUDE

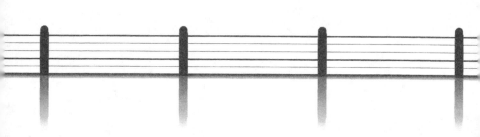

CHAPTER EIGHTEEN

THE DOMAIN
OF DRUDGERY

It does require the supernatural grace of God to live twenty-four hours
in every day as a saint, to go through drudgery as a disciple, to live an
ordinary, unobserved, ignored existence as a disciple of Jesus. It is inbred
in us that we have to do exceptional things for God; but we [do] not.
We have to be exceptional in the ordinary things, to be holy in
mean streets, among mean people, and this is not learned in five minutes.

Oswald Chambers

Someone has said that the definition of insanity is to continue to
do the same thing over and over but expecting it to yield different results. I thought of this when the kids and I got Lee a
Yankee Flipper for his birthday.

We had been having trouble with squirrels leaping onto our former bird feeder and gorging themselves. Designed to thwart squirrels, the Yankee Flipper is a clear, vertical cylinder that you fill with
seed; at the bottom is a circular metal perch for the birds to stand
on as they feed. This round perch is connected to a powerful, bat-
tery-charged motor. A bird's feathered weight is not enough to
engage the motor. But if a fat, larcenous squirrel jumps up on the
perch, its weight trips the motor, which spins the perch in a violent
rotation. The idea is that the squirrel then finds himself flung off

171

the feeder and sailing through the air rather than eating birdseed, which had been his expectation.

We charged up the Yankee Flipper's battery. We filled it with tempting seed and hung it from a trellis on our deck, which is about a story and a half above the ground. Then the children reluctantly went to school and Lee to work: I alone was left to watch the Yankee Flipper. My home office computer station just happens to face that part of the deck.

The birds loved it. They perched and warbled and ate quite happily. Then the first fat cad of a squirrel appeared, bounding confidently across the deck and up onto the railing just below the feeder. I held my breath. He threw one self-assured paw onto the perch and prepared to hoist himself onto it, hungry for brunch. The perch whirled and the squirrel twirled. He landed on the deck railing.

He marched back to the feeder. This time he jumped and all four feet landed on the perch. It spun wildly, and the squirrel spiraled out into midair off the deck, his mouth open in a little "o," his paws flung wide. Then there was a thud, and he landed somewhere in the backyard.

By now I had my nose pressed against the window. Other squirrels hopped up onto the railing, hungry to prove their superiority over the stunned squirrel now lying prone in the yard. They leapt onto the Yankee Flipper. It spun, they flew. "Incoming!" I shouted out the window; a barrage of squirrels crashed on the grass.

The first squirrel crawled up the deck steps and back under the feeder, his jump onto it a little more rickety than before. The mechanism tripped, and again he went flying out in a lovely arc, orbiting the back yard.

He dragged himself slowly back, a mad glint in his eye. He hobbled to the feeder, determined that things would go differently this time. He placed his paws on the perch . . . and flew again.

Aside from his being the best entertainment I'd had in weeks, I saw myself in that mad squirrel. How many times have I done the same thing, over and over, vainly hoping that it would bring different results? How many times have I started a stressful day determined that it would turn out differently than the bad day before . . . even though I haven't changed my strategy?

Living with a habitually grateful heart requires that we change strategy. It requires us to change how we respond to life's stimuli— lest we end up like that battered squirrel flying off the wheel, again and again.

Now, it can be easier, relatively speaking, to perceive life through the lens of gratitude in out-of-the-ordinary situations. Certainly that's true on missions trips, life's milestone moments, or lovely times like our visit to Romania. It can even be true in tragedies: there seems to be a certain spiritual adrenaline that fuels the fires of faith in times of crisis. Often—though not always—we sense God's power and presence during catastrophes. We feel that there is grace to help in the times of great need.

But what about the everyday life, when there is no big picture, when it's life on the small screen, where the same old triggers are there, charged and waiting to trip us up?

The fact is, the spiritual perspective that bears us up in extraordinary emergencies is also available in the dreariest chores of daily existence . . . in the mundane challenges of business meetings, carpools, homework, family frustrations, daily maintenance—all those necessary, repetitive, sometimes distasteful responsibilities that make up the bulk of our lives.

As Oswald Chambers said, it requires supernatural grace to live ordinary life well.

> Drudgery is the touchstone of character. . . . There are times when there is no . . . thrill, but just the daily round, the common task. . . . Do not expect God always to give you His thrilling minutes, but learn to live in the domain of drudgery by the power of God.[1]

God gives us what we need to live by His power even as we slog through the bogs. So in these closing chapters, I want to explore everyday gratitude, and the "how" of it.

We've talked about *what* to remember, for example, but *how* do we trigger the habit of remembering? There are practical things we can do to cultivate a grateful heart, simple ways to shape our perceptions so we see daily wonders in the domain of drudgery. These hold the keys to the secret of responding to the same old stimuli in new ways . . . so we experience different results than just life as usual.

CHAPTER NINETEEN

MEMORY ROCKS

When asked if my cup is half-full or half-empty,
my only response is that I am thankful I have a cup.
Sam Lefkowitz

Here I raise my Ebenezer;
Hither by Thy help I'm come;
And I hope, by Thy good pleasure,
Safely to arrive at home.
Robert Robinson, "Come, Thou Fount
of Every Blessing," 1758

The first practical tool for everyday gratitude is so simple it's been used since the Stone Age. It doesn't require technology ... no Blackberry, laptop, cell phone, software. No special seminars or advanced degrees. We just need to pay attention to rocks—and other natural reminders of God's supernatural faithfulness.

As we said earlier, remembering doesn't come naturally. Satan will tempt us to forget God's faithfulness. That's why we must take action and build up Ebenezers: visible, physical reminders of invisible, spiritual truths.

We must tie a string around our index finger, so to speak, so that in the midst of daily stress, we'll remember what's real. As we'll consider in chapter 21, whether it's a page jotted in a journal, dates noted in a Bible margin, letters, photographs, calendars, trees planted deep, flags raised high, mementos in a glass case—or, as in biblical times, ordinary rocks—such tools can remind us of who God is and what He has done. They are witnesses from the past to give us confidence for the present: God is reliable. He can be trusted. He is with us.

Old Testament Jews piled up stones of remembrance. While they were fighting their way into the Promised Land, they met many enemies stronger than themselves. At one point the people had gathered at the town of Mizpah, just north of Jerusalem. Their leader, Samuel, offered a sacrifice to God, crying out for His help. The Philistine army was advancing—and they had the military power to grind the Israelites into the dust.

But God had promised to protect His people when they were obedient to their covenant with Him. He intervened. As the Philistines marched toward Mizpah, the skies exploded with ear-splitting peals of roaring thunder that rattled their armor and shook their hearts. They fled, with the Israelites pouring out of the city, pursuing and slaughtering them as they routed.

The Israelites could not have won this battle without help. And lest they forget the miracle, lest their gratitude wane, Samuel made a monument. He took a large stone, set it up outside of Mizpah, and named it *Ebenezer*, which means, in the original Hebrew, "Thus far has the LORD helped us."[1]

Aside from causing generations of earnest hymn-singing children great confusion ("Here I raise my Ebenezer" ... "Dad, just what, exactly, *is* an Ebenezer?"), this stone sets a state of mind for those who follow God today. "Thus far" the Lord has helped us.

Inherent in that phrase is the truth that God aids us, intervenes for us, and is with us just as far as we've been on the journey. We have His promise for tomorrow, yes, but we're given no reassuring DVD that will show us exactly *how* the story will turn out, precisely *how* He'll help us tomorrow, or next week, or next year. If we had such visual assurance, we'd need no faith.

We're not to worry about the future. The fact is, thus far the Lord has helped us. And tomorrow He will help us thus far again. Like the manna God gave the Jews in the desert, God's help is daily bread. We can't store it up for the future. We look for it one day at a time.

Like Samuel, the biblical leader Joshua used stones as natural reminders of God's supernatural help. As the children of Israel began their conquest of the Promised Land, their first obstacle was its boundary: the swift, freezing, flooded Jordan River. It was impassable. But God had been talking to Joshua, and against all odds, Joshua believed Him. He called the people together, the priests carrying the Ark of the Covenant at the head of the assembly. As soon as the priests carrying the Ark set foot in the Jordan, he told them, its waters flowing downstream will be cut off.

Note the order of events. The priests had to move forward, advancing on the river, which were still flowing freely. If God had stopped the waters first, the priests and people would need no faith. Resolute, the men marched forward ... and as they did, the swollen river stopped, blocked, in fact, at a town that was seventeen miles upstream. The priests marched across the dry riverbed, confused fish flopping everywhere, followed by every man, woman, and child in the nation of Israel.

After they were all safely across, Joshua called for representatives from each tribe to hoist big boulders from the middle of the river bed. Later, after the Jordan's waters had rushed back, flowing at flood stage again, he used these river-smoothed stones to build an enduring monument. Why? So "in the future, when your children ask you, 'What do these stones mean?' tell them that the flow of the Jordan was cut off.... These stones are to be a memorial to the people of Israel forever."[2]

Significantly, that memorial was not only a reminder of God's miracle at the Jordan, but also of His similar miracle forty years earlier. A double Ebenezer. God did to the Jordan "just what he had done to the Red Sea when he dried it up," Joshua told the people—so they might always fear and revere the God whose power could stop rushing waters whenever He pleased.[3]

God does the miracles. We make the markers so we remember to trust Him for more. In the same way that gravestones mark the memories of the dead, or monuments memorialize heroic deeds, ordinary rocks can serve as tangible reminders of what God did at a certain point in time, and thus link us to spiritual truths about who He is.

Years ago, I brought my own rock back from the land of Joshua and the Jordan. Every pilgrim and tourist I know has done the same. It's a wonder the Holy Land isn't stripped bare by now.

My rock is from the Dead Sea. I picked it up from the shore as a remembrance of this place whose sheer strangeness bent my brain. It is the lowest site on earth. Though springs and the Jordan River flow into it, nothing flows out. Its waters are almost 33 percent salt. King Herod dipped here; Queen Cleopatra imported Dead Sea mud for spa treatments. People do the same today. The black sludge is used for migraines, arthritis, and wrinkles. Pillars of salt line the Dead Sea shores like icebergs or replicas of Lot's wife, for whom migraines became moot.

I picked my way through this moonscape to the warm water, waded further in, and floated, my body impossibly buoyant. I lay on my side, one arm behind my head like a mermaid, then sat as if in a chair, then floated vertically. It was eerie and wonderful, as in dreams where one can fly.

I emerged from the strange waters onto the rocky shore. There are showers on the beach so you can immediately rinse the brine from your body, lest you pickle. I showered, bent, and there was my rock. It is today as it was in 1981 when I found it: a pink, smooth stone, utterly self-contained, at home on my desk as it was in the land that hosted God when He walked on earth.

And that is why larcenous people like me remove rocks from Israel. When we see the earth where Jesus trod, we want a piece of the action. We want to fit our feet into His footprints, feel the stones He must have skipped across the waters. He stood right here, perhaps. His boat must have come ashore right here. The Incarnation becomes not just an idea, but a reality I can almost see. Here is where it happened.

Some say the crucifixion took place on the big skull-shaped rock that rises now above the Arab bus station. I stood there. The cries of the roadside vendors, the idling engines, and the smell of diesel fumes all fell away. I could sense the big cross stark against the sky, His body lifted up for all to see ... and later, buried. Whether it was on the site of the Church of the Holy Sepulcher, where pilgrims shove to kiss the blessed stone upon which the cross was set, or in the relative quiet of the Garden Tomb, or somewhere close by, it happened. I could feel it in the earth, smell it in the air: here, right near here, He sprang from the tomb, Lord of the Dance irrepressible.

During that long-ago April journey to Jerusalem, my friend Patti and I kept vigil through the night before Easter dawn. Earlier that evening, we had walked with our backpacks out of our lodging in the village of Ein Karem. West of Jerusalem, Ein Karem was once the home of John the Baptist. Now it is home to a Catholic seminary. Patti's uncle, Father Pete, was in charge, and Patti and I were hosted there by twenty-six priests-in-training.

We climbed up the hill by the light of the rising moon and caught a little cab called a *sheroot* to the Old City. The streets were quiet, but when we arrived at the cathedral of St. Anne's, crowds of believers filled the ancient church. Their voices, from many nations, swelled as one: *Alleluia! Alleluia!*

We went with some of the brothers to a vigil near the site of Pontius Pilate's sentencing of Christ. Nuns served us coffee and cake. Now high in the sky, the full moon shone on the golden Dome of the Rock, just out the window. At three in the morning came the Moslem call to prayer, amplified by loudspeakers, echoing in the night.

After, the quiet was even more pronounced. Something was about to happen, two thousand years before. We walked through covered streets to the church of "St. Peter in Gallicantu," a poetic rendering of "St. Peter and the Cock Crowing." It was almost time for modern cocks to crow, and for modern Peters like us to revel in the Resurrection. We passed out of the city and climbed a rocky hill to wait for the sun to rise over Jerusalem. When it did, we were beside ourselves, outside ourselves, laughing with sheer joy. An old man in a nightcap clapped open his window, stuck his head out, and scowled at us.

Later, when the market opened at six, we bought warm sesame bread. A toothless Arab lady selling green almonds grinned and gave us a few. We scattered their shells as we walked; the stones of the city shone as the sun grew strong and a fresh wind blew. Christ is risen indeed.

My parents went to Israel a few years after that. They went to Masada, the great Herodian fortress built into the rock cliffs that tower above the Dead Sea. In AD 66 a group of Jewish rebels took over the fortress from the Romans who were garrisoned there. After the fall of Jerusalem and the destruction of the Temple in 70, they were joined by more Jewish zealots.

By late 73, the Romans had finally had enough. The entire Tenth Legion marched on Masada. The soldiers established camps at the base of the cliffs and laid siege. They built a rampart of thousands of tons of stones and earth. When spring arrived, they rolled battering rams and catapults up the dusty ramp. They breached Masada's mighty wall.

In the dark night before the dawn attack that would bring their end, the Jewish zealots laid their plans. They knew what would happen. After the slaughter, some of them would survive to be marched in chains through the streets of Rome. Their wives and children who were not killed would become whores and slaves.

So the Jews made a gruesome choice that would rob the Romans of their victory. They cast lots to determine ten of their number who would serve as executioners. They lay down in family groups. The executioners dispatched each family. Then the ten cast lots again, and one slew the other nine. Then the last man set fire to the complex—except for the food stores, so the Romans would know that their motive was not starvation—and fell upon his own sword.

The historian Josephus says that when the Romans broke through the next morning, their heavy armor jingling as they climbed up ladders and flooded over the walls of the fortress, swords drawn, they were met only by an overwhelming silence . . . and the still bodies of 960 Jews who chose to die rather than be taken by Rome.

Two Jewish women had hidden in a cistern. They survived the bloody night and the Roman morning, and their account is part of Josephus's historic record. Masada was painstakingly excavated in the early 1960s by the Israeli military hero and archaeologist Yigael Yadin. He found the intact skeletons of some of the defenders; these were buried with full military honors in 1969. Today the fortress stands as a testimony to the power of towering stone, and the fact that even when strong rocks are breached, the human spirit is not.

My mother brought back a stone from Masada. It is white and worn, little more than a pebble. And now, when I take it out of the green velvet box in which she tucked her treasures, I find that it does not look very different from all that is left of Mom. Her ashes too are crumbled, tumbled bits of bone that look like stone.

Like their grandmother, my children collect rocks. As of yet, they have no need for exotic travels, for they are not particular about their stones' origins. Rocks from our back yard are good; so are stones from the creek behind our house. We also like to explore the woods and cliffs near the Potomac River. Whenever we return from a hike, Walker's pockets are full of stones. If he fell in the river, he would sink like Virginia Woolf in the opening scenes of the *Mrs. Dalloway* film, but that is not his intention. He just loves rocks.

We often climb to the top of the cliffs near Great Falls. The river flows far below. We can see history in the striated rock of the canyon. George Washington stood here, surveying the Potowmack, as he called it. Algonquian Indians hunted in these woods and fished in this river. The water's power has thundered and cut, smoothing and shaping the big gorge. Hurricanes come; the river floods. And still the rocks remain, strong bones of the durable earth.

The landscape is yet a bit wild; we sometimes pretend we are trekking to Mordor. When we stay connected to reality we see the red or blue belay ropes of climbers, with their bright helmets and Spiderman costumes, bouncing down the rock face. Straining on his leash, Lewis the labradoodle barks to them, encouragingly. Far below, in the river, kayakers spin in the roiling waters.

We come home, dirty and gratified, the dog full of beans because he thinks he is a mountain goat. I make the children check their rocks at the front door, like a security guard screening passengers for the metal detector. We go inside to wash the river mud off our arms; unlike the Dead Sea sludge, it has no great healing powers.

The rocks wait outside on the porch. Rocks are patient. Later, some of them end up inside, on Walker's bookshelf near a muddy bird nest and other treasures, or on my own desk, near their exotic sister stone from the far side of the sea.

My Potomac River rocks are touchstones to sunny days with our children, who will soon be grown and gone. They prompt waves of gratitude to God: thank You. Life is precious. Life is sweet. It thunders by so fast, a waterfall pulled by the gravity of time, rushing toward the end of these days as I know them.

Rocks matter. Their matter is mineral, some of the same minerals I ingest in my morning vitamin. Iron. Phosphorus. Magnesium. Zinc. Copper. I have more in common with common rocks than I had realized—though I was made in the image of One who calls Himself "the Rock of Israel," the "Rock and ... Redeemer," "the Rock eternal." "Look to the rock from which you were cut and to the quarry from which you were hewn," He says.[4]

But as elemental as rocks are, Ebenezers needn't always be stones. They can take all kinds of forms. In fact, depending on the complexity of our experiences, a rock of remembrance can be as simple as a doorknob. It is for Commander Paul Galanti, a bomber pilot who was shot down over North Vietnam one summer day in 1966.

CHAPTER TWENTY

"GOOD NIGHT AND GOD BLESS"

Name: Paul Edward Galanti
Rank/Branch: 03/United States Navy/pilot
Date of Loss: 17 June 1966
Country of Loss: North Vietnam
Loss Coordinates: 191500N 1054600E
Status: Returnee
Missions: 97
Aircraft/Vehicle/Ground A4C #149528

What does it feel like to eject from a fighter aircraft streaking through the sky at nearly 600 miles per hour?

Evidently most people who have done it don't remember . . . or they don't survive.

For his part, Commander Paul Galanti doesn't quite recall how it felt that summer day in 1966 when his aircraft took North Vietnamese antiaircraft fire and fell in a flaming spiral to earth. Everything happened too fast.

Paul Galanti was a graduate of the U.S. Naval Academy, cocky, courageous, and like most twenty-six-year-olds, invincible. He and three other pilots had just completed their bombing mission on that June morning, taking out a railroad siding about 160 miles from Hanoi. His Douglas A4 Skyhawk was a single-seat jet flown by both land-based and carrier squadrons, the Navy's standard light attack aircraft, affectionately called the "Scooter" by its pilots.

The weather was bad. Then, in one second, there was a staccato rapping sound and shuddering vibrations rocked the plane. It lost electrical power, rolled, shook, and shattered. Thick black smoke poured from the air-conditioning vents; the tail fell in pieces through the clouds.

Paul radioed the other pilots. "I'm hit!" he shouted. He reached up and jerked the ejection face curtain over his head. The canopy blew off, the rocket fired with an enormous crack, and he flew out of the flaming plane. The force yanked him out, down, then up with a savage jerk as his parachute, thankfully, opened.

There was a sea breeze blowing from the east that day. Normally the wind blew from the west, which would have carried Paul Galanti's parachute out over the Gulf of Tonkin and toward the rescue destroyer, which he could see in the waters below. He could see the Sea Sprite helicopter on its deck, ready to lift off and come get him.

But the wind from the east was carrying him inland, right into enemy territory. The front of his flight suit was sticky and red. Paul hadn't even noticed getting shot, but a bullet had taken a big chunk of flesh out of his neck. Blood was everywhere.

The ground was drawing nearer. He hit the beach, knees buckling, trying to get to some scrubby bushes for cover. He could hear North Vietnamese soldiers coming. He made one last transmission before he smashed his radio into pieces with a rock. "Send the helo back," he yelled. "They're too close and they'll get it! See you guys after the war."

The enemy advanced on him, rifles in hand. Paul's pistol was on his hip, but he raised his hands in the air and stood up slowly, deliberately. He didn't want to spook the soldiers; some of the young ones were wild-eyed, ready to shoot. They rushed on him, tied him to a tree, then lined up like a firing squad. An older officer yelled at them to stop. The American pilot was more valuable to them alive.

The march north to Hanoi took twelve days. Paul was blind-folded, handcuffed, moved only at night to avoid being spotted by American bombers or rescue helicopters. Villagers would follow him on the trail, throwing sticks and rocks. Paul knew he had to get away before he got to prison; there would be little chance of escape afterward. But he had no idea where he was.

They arrived in Hanoi. U.S. forces had not bombed the city or a twenty-five-mile radius around it before this point in the war, but now bombs were falling—though not on the infamous Hanoi Hilton, a triangular prison spreading across a city block, sur-rounded by a dry moat and twenty-foot walls studded with shards of glass and topped with electrified barbed wire.

Paul was put in a seven-by-seven-foot cell with two concrete slabs for beds. There were bloodstains on the dirty, whitewashed walls. The door was made of heavy, dark wood. It had big, rusty bolts, an immense lock, and a peephole window about halfway up.

Paul would stare at it, and other locked doors like it, for nearly seven years.

He was stripped of his filthy flight suit and given some thin, faded cotton pajamas to wear. Twice a day he was issued greasy, watery "soup" with a lump of pig fat in it. Occasionally there was stale bread, abrasive with bits of sand and dirt.

The North Vietnamese were distracted by the constant bomb-ings. So another American prisoner, Colonel Robbie Risner, who had been brought back to the cell block for more torture, was able to whisper to Paul in the night. Risner taught him how to commu-nicate with his fellow captured pilots. The tap code was a cipher in which the alphabet was transposed into a five by five dot matrix. Each letter was represented by the placement of taps on the cell wall. The prisoners' taps on the bloody walls became their lifeline to one another.

Every Sunday Paul would hear the muffled knocks . . . and like his military brothers he could not see, he would stand up, face toward the United States, and say the Lord's Prayer and the Pledge of Allegiance, his hand over his heart. As the days and weeks went by, he would stare at his locked cell door and remember scenes from the past . . . like his first day of flight training. The instructor had been tough, bigger than life with his narrow waist and broad, strong shoulders.

"Look at the man to your right, and to your left, and then yourself," he had barked one day as Paul and the others stood in formation. "One of the three of you will be dead in five years." Optimists all, each had wondered which of the *other* two guys it would be.

Now, in his cell, Paul still had hope . . . though he was always hungry, sweltering, or freezing depending on the season, pacing in his tiny cell. Escape or deliverance didn't look like a live option. But he wasn't dead yet. So he remained guardedly positive.

And every night the knocks would come. *GN.* Good night. *GB.* God bless.

Then came the day that Paul was pulled out of his cell and thrown into an interrogation room. It was winter, bitter cold. The only thing in the room was a wooden stool. The guards shoved Paul onto it, his wrists handcuffed taut behind his back. He sat like this for hours. Late that night, his head nodded, eyes closing, but every time he drifted toward sleep, the guard would beat Paul with his heavy rifle butt.

Paul lost track of time. As the days and nights unfolded, the room spun, the repeated blows to his head bled, trickling down his neck, his arms still pinioned behind his back like drumsticks. He could feel his life ebbing away. "I'm not going to make it," he thought, his eyes crossing, the locked door before him fading in and out of his sight.

Then it happened. Paul slumped on the stool, helpless, and a figure walked through the prison wall. He came to Paul, touched him on the shoulder. *Paul. I am with you. You are going to be all right.*

Paul had never seen him before. But he knew who He was.

A little later, the guards unlocked the door to Paul's cell. They pulled him off the stool, dragged him to a regular cell, and gave him warm clothes. He slept, and survived.

Paul Galanti returned home from the war in 1973, after 2,432 days of captivity in North Vietnam. His wife, who had championed his cause during his absence, was waiting for him. (Others were waiting too. The very first letter Paul received at home was from the Internal Revenue Service. *We realize that you've had extenuating circumstances*, the IRS informed the POW, *but you haven't paid your taxes since 1967*.)

The Galantis went on to have two children. Paul went to Navy flight refresher training; after finishing his military career he excelled in various business venues. Today he is an active executive in his sixties, his youthful cockiness mellowed into mature conviction about just what is important and what is not.[1]

"When I got home from Vietnam," he says, "many Americans were endlessly complaining. They complained about nearly everything. The motto, *unity over self*, that had effectively held our POWs together under difficult circumstances, seemed to have been replaced at home with the first-person singular: *me, myself, and I*."

But to Paul and his fellow POWs, life's simple blessings were not to be taken for granted. Having a hot meal, a warm bed, time with friends and family, and the ability to make choices, to do anything they wanted, were visions they had dreamed of for years, during torture, filth, hunger, handcuffs, and prison bars.

Paul's perspective today is simple. Everywhere he goes, there are ordinary reminders of the difference between prison and living free. "Here's the deal," he'll say, his blue eyes clear, his tone matter-of-fact, "Every day that you've got a doorknob—on *your* side of the door—is a day to be thankful."

CHAPTER TWENTY-ONE

EBENEZERS EVERYWHERE

Gratitude is born in hearts that take time
to count up past mercies.

Charles Jefferson

Few of us have had experiences like Paul Galanti's. But ever since I met him, I don't take doorknobs for granted any more. Now they remind me that liberty is sweet indeed.

Doorknobs aside, there are all kinds of other Ebenezers that can prompt us to remember spiritual truths.

A friend keeps an old suitcase near her front door. It reminds her that this world is not her home, she's just a-passin' through. She is packed, so to speak, and ready to go Home whenever God initiates those travel plans.

An Ebenezer can be a piece of jewelry. The other morning at the breakfast table I noticed a blue bracelet on Emily's ankle. "Where did that come from?" I asked.

Haley responded before Emily could speak, a rather uncommon occurrence.

"It's Right-Way Jonah!"

Emily had been a junior counselor at Vacation Bible School six months earlier. The blue bubble bracelet she had worn ever since was a connection to the story of Jonah, who initially ran the wrong way when God told him to do something he did not care to do. As you recall, Jonah's consequences were not pleasant. The little blue band was a reminder, an Ebenezer for little people to go the right way when God calls. Half a year later, eight year-old Haley remembered. (Though for my part, I was left wondering how I could go for six months without regarding my daughter's ankle.)

Friends who live nearby planted a tree in memory of their young daughter who died. Not that they would forget her ... but the slender, growing maple in their front yard is a physical reminder that though their little girl is with them no more, she lives—and they will see her again. When neighbors pass by on a crisp fall day and see the glowing golden maple, it is more than a tree. It's an Ebenezer: even in loss and sorrow, God is with us, and He is good.

Recently I was in a fourteenth-century Orthodox cathedral in Transylvania. Off the main entrance to the transept was a narrow hallway filled with paintings. I headed down it, followed by a tiny, ancient caretaker lady who had seemingly popped out of a recess in the stone walls. She pointed out picture after picture. Here was one of a little girl with braids and pink bows, lying beneath the wheel of a 1940-era car. Here was a man lying pale and gaunt on a hospital bed. Here was a young man bleeding after a fall from a roof. There were dozens of similar paintings that had been given to the church by people who wanted to honor God's intervention in their lives. The little girl with the braids had recovered. The man in the hospital bed had gotten better. The bloody boy had healed.

I pointed to a picture of a heavily loaded farm cart. A stout horse stood in its traces, and a man lay crushed under its wheels. "What about this one?" I asked. "Did he live?"

"No," the wrinkled woman replied. "But his family was so grateful that he died right away. He did not suffer."

Back at home, far from the cathedral hallway of Ebenezers, a friend told me about some icons of his own. His brother had digitized a bunch of old photographs from their childhood. My friend loaded them on his PC and clicked through forgotten images of his youth. The photos weren't extraordinary: a new, red bike. A camping trip, featuring an impossibly small pup tent. A cookout. Ordinary moments—but they were tangible connections to a childhood that was no more, and as he viewed the images, Ken became conscious of a cascade of gratitude coursing through him. He had not had a perfect youth—but in those forgotten photos, he saw a clear trail of evidence of God's faithfulness. It made him smile.

I smile too when I look back at my own visual record. Sometimes I get a little distracted when I regard photos from college and wonder why, just why, the currency of my youth was spent in a decade degraded by polyester, platform shoes, and enormous bellbottoms.

Such concerns aside, however, I look back and give thanks. In spite of myself, I survived college and graduate school. That is testimony alone to God's faithfulness to me, particularly during times I was not faithful to Him.

Sometimes I look at far older photos, black-and-white images of myself at four, an earnest, curly-haired flower girl clutching her white basket of rose petals. I remember taking my job at my much-older brother's wedding quite seriously. Whenever petals landed awry, I'd bend and set them right. It took me a long time to make my way down the long red aisle, past all the pews, my tidy track of pastel petals trailing straight behind me.

Many times over the years I chose weeds rather than fragrant flowers or got caught in thickets of thorns. But by God's grace, I eventually arrived at my own wedding march. I flip open our heavy leather album and look at the fine photographs, bordered in gold. There are the friends who stood with us, the pastors who sealed us, the family that supported us. My parents and other loved ones who served as witnesses that day have since passed on. We remember them. I smooth the photos, and sometimes they bring me to tears. God has been faithful.

I have a smaller book in a drawer. It is bound in leatherette, clasped by a tiny metal lock whose gold finish rubbed off long ago.

It is my sixth-grade diary. The other day I flipped through it, amazed that the girl in its pages was so like my daughters. The past and present blur, but the point is clear: thus far, even as I write this paragraph, the Lord has helped me. (And, should I ever finish writing this book, let its pages testify to that truth again: God is faithful.)

Many friends are far more faithful journalists than I am. But the point is, whether in lovely prayer journals or in coffee-stained spiral-bound notebooks, on scraps of cocktail napkins, or emails to others that we print and save, we must create a written record. One need not be a "writer" to do this. It is simply imperative to write down what God has done, so we can look back and remember, and give lavish thanks to Him. This glorifies God. It increases our faith and strengthens our vitality.

A friend began keeping a gratitude journal a year ago. It was nothing fancy, no eloquent tome. She simply jotted five things each day for which she was thankful. Some items were large, others small . . . anything from disasters averted, to sunsets enjoyed, to the grace to hold her tongue in a tough situation. She was simply being intentional about thanking God.

This little habit had huge results. My friend found that the more she practiced gratitude, the more gratitude she had to practice. The habit of expressing thanks to God each day was like a pair of prescription lenses that sharpened her vision. The more she thanked, the more she saw. She began to perceive God at work in situations where His presence had been cloaked to her before. The simple habit of thanking God became a ladder to living on a new plane altogether.

As my friend's example shows, making Ebenezers does not require sophisticated techniques. It simply entails practicing small habits purposefully.

Another useful tool toward that end is music. When my disheartened feelings do not match the great truths I know in my head, I have found that the greatest offensive action I can take is to sing.

This can indeed be offensive to others, for I am no great singer. But I do know that when my soul is corroded and cold, if I open my rusty lips and sing the songs of the saints who have gone before, their "psalms and hymns and spiritual songs . . . always giving thanks to God," as Ephesians 5 says, something happens. My soul warms, loosens, draws near to God. And He draws near to me.

Similarly, friends can be Ebenezers as they remind us of God's faithfulness. For nearly twenty years, Lee and I have been part of a group of couples who meet for dinner once a month. When we started doing this, none of us had children. Now there is a tribe. Over Mexican food, or Italian, or marinated pork tenderloin on the grill, we talk—quite wittily, we think—about politics and movies and books and issues.

We brainstorm about our children's needs, our bemused reactions to the aging process, or other crises. Since we have years of history together, we can remind one another of God's help thus far on the journey. We've gone to each other's parents' funerals, prayed through job changes, military duty, and more emergencies than we care to recall. We occasionally take the party out of town. One New Year's day, two of our number, intent on becoming members of the Polar Bear Club, sprinted across frozen sand into the Atlantic Ocean. In the snow. The rest of us watched from a glass-sided, heated indoor pool. We miss them.

Those years of supper-club history is a great thing. I have an even older Ebenezer, my best friend Patti, who proves her friendship by allowing me to call her "an even older Ebenezer." God made Patti with a huge laugh and a buoyant spirit, irrepressible creativity, and a tenacious willingness to dig down to the real truth of things. Talking with her is like having your back scratched, long and luxuriously.

Patti and I lived across the street from each another when we were young. One day when we were fourteen, we perched in the upper branches of a big sycamore tree in my side yard. There we felt our high calling, that God had knit our hearts together as friends forever. We climbed down and commenced the rest of our lives. We communed through the dramas of junior and senior high school, roomed together in college and graduate school, wearing one another's clothes for the duration. Hers were always better.

I remember riding our bikes into DC on my fifteenth birthday, the golden ginkgo trees on Georgetown's cobblestone side streets, the arching skies blue above. I remember riding in the limousines that carried us to one another's weddings, the smooth, white satin of our dresses billowing around us. I remember riding in another limo, looking through the back window to a long line of cars following us, their headlights on. We could barely comprehend we were in a procession to the cemetery where we would bury Patti's husband, father to her three small girls, killed by cancer at thirty-eight. I remember the day after that, kneeling with Patti in her big closet as she clutched the empty sleeves of John's big suits and cried his name. We hugged in a heap; I had not the remotest clue of what to say.

In the years since then, we've said a lot. With varying degrees of wisdom we've prayed and cried and fought and laughed. The friendship has proven its resilient strength. It is a silver web whose cords are not easily broken.

And as we get older, we find that one of us has forgotten key details of some adventures and events, and the other has forgotten complementary ones. It is kind of God to harmonize our amnesia. We share a common memory, its pieces fitting together to remind us what really matters. It is Christ, the love of Christ, the grace of Christ. Christ alone. We serve as mirrored Ebenezers to one another of God's faithfulness: look, I'm still here! So are you! And if we've made it this far, bedraggled and worn, still calling on the name of Jesus, God is indeed faithful!

Whether one is fortunate enough to have a Patti or not, we must connect with others in order to remember well. Apart from finding ourselves in solitary confinement, stranded on an unpeopled continent, or in similarly rare situations, we must plant ourselves in a community of believers. As we said in chapter 17, friends in Christ can prompt one another to remember His goodness. This is particularly important since we live in a land whose daily values tempt us to covetously compare ourselves with those who have more. Friends can pitch buckets of cold water on each other's heads—literally, if need be—to jolt one another back to what is Real.

And it is in the community of believers that we center around the greatest Ebenezer of all: the Lord's Supper. As we said in chapter 14, the Greek root of *eucharist* means "to be grateful." The communion points us back in time. Gathered around the table, in the taking of the cup—in whatever tradition we do so—we remember the Lord's death until He comes again. We remember that He poured out His blood and gave His Body to pay for our sins, so we would not wander in this world frozen by fear and guilt, nor forever burn in the fires of hell. We know that so well—but the great danger is that we forget its essence. Apart from Christ's pardon for our debt, we are as far from Him as a Hitler or a Hussein.

In my own home church, I draw near with others to remember that truth. We weep; in the community of close friends we realize the sweet-sharp abundance of grace.

And at the communion table in faraway places, I remember that Christ binds me forever with friends abroad. Once I was in a packed church in Havana, where ceiling fans turned and Caribbean breezes blew in the open windows. I was with a group of travelers from the U.S.; oddly enough, one of our number had died the day before. She had an incurable illness that was far more advanced than she—and we—had realized.

Needless to say, we were shocked, and her unexpected departure for heaven colored our perceptions of the communion celebration. I watched as our Cuban brothers and sisters came down the church's long center aisle, bearing the bread and wine, led by dancers holding huge banners aloft: *Pan de vida*. Bread of life. *Vino nuevo*. New wine. In the midst of the procession came their minister, black and red vestments flowing behind him, shepherd of the flock.

"What is life?" he called to the people. "What will be left of my life? We don't know when it will end . . . this is the moment to put our lives in front of God, and consider what fruits they are bearing for Him."

Many of the Cubans were weeping in their pews.

"*Resurreccion!*" they sang.

"I am the Resurrection and the Life . . . he who believes in Me will live, even though he dies; and whoever lives and believes in Me will never die . . ."

Then, as the pastor read Psalm 23, we took communion two by two, North Americans and Cubans celebrating the body and blood of Christ. As "my" Cuban met me at the front, we smiled, took our small cups together and tilted our heads toward heaven, drinking deep of Jesus. Then we went our separate ways. I will see her again in paradise.

As with the Eucharistic meal, we celebrate many Ebenezers on purpose, taking the initiative, out of obedience, to set them up. There are other Ebenezers, more mysterious, that God sometimes wafts our way on the breath of a wind . . . a smell, taste, touch, song . . . an unexpected, sensual remembrance of things past that lures us to be grateful for His goodness.

CHAPTER TWENTY-TWO

PLEASURES DU JOUR

Nothing tastes.

Marie Antoinette

What am I grateful for? Let me see . . . I really appreciate quiet,
a hot shower and a warm bed, all of which I have here. I'm grateful
that my children love and care about me and that I have the ability
to communicate with them on a regular basis; I'm grateful for friends
and family who care about me and enrich my life; I'm grateful
that most of the bad guys in Iraq haven't gotten around to trying
to kill me personally; but most of all, I'm grateful for the occasional
fresh asparagus that comes our way.

email from a contractor friend

working in Baghdad, April 2004

During graduate school years ago, I passed through a French
phase of my life. I read Proust, Baudelaire, Flaubert, and other
Gallic writers in their original tongue. I waited tables in a rustic
café. I traveled to Paris and chatted in French with my hosts. I consumed crepes, cornichons, escargots.

Now I have forgotten it all: the French, the Eiffel Tower, the
snails, and most certainly the Proust . . . except for one small thing.

In his *À la Recherche du Temps Perdu*, or *Remembrance of
Things Past*—most of which I have no remembrance—Proust
wrote about how he could not willfully bring to mind certain

images of his early life. He could not pull them up on the screen of his mind by simply hitting an "open files" button, so to speak. Memories came only if they were called up by *sensory* triggers. So a *madeleine*, a French tea cookie, served as a connector to forgotten memories of his childhood.

> And as soon as I had recognized the taste of the piece of madeleine . . . immediately the old grey house upon the street . . . rose up like a stage set to attach itself to the little pavilion opening on to the garden which had been built out behind it . . . and with the house the town, from morning to night and in all weathers, the square where I used to be sent before lunch, the streets along which I used to run errands, the country roads we took when it was fine.[1]

Many of us have experienced the same phenomenon.

The other day I found a bottle of my mother's perfume, an old-fashioned scent called Nina Ricci. I carefully pulled off the golden cap and sprayed its mist into the air, hesitant because I knew it would make me cry. I breathed in the fragrance, and my mother's presence enveloped me like an embrace. And then she was gone.

The same thing happens if I get a whiff of sheets dried on a clothesline, or the scent of Ivory Snow. My mother returns, for the fold of a second, her hug almost real in the freshness of clean, sun-warmed laundry.

There are other remembrances of things past that are stirred up by a smell. The whiff of sea salt and baked wooden boardwalk takes me to summer days at the ocean when I was eight. The smell makes me feel the sand in my pigtails. The smell of diesel fuel makes me smile, for it makes me remember an idling bus. My friends and I climbed aboard, and it took us all the way from Virginia to Young Life camp in the mountains of Colorado.

Any number of odors take me directly to my childhood, no effort required. So I sent out an email asking a few friends to tell me about smells from their own lost youth. These are busy people. But the question was evocative enough to push other things aside, for I received a flood of replies raving about everything from tomato vines to saddle polish to fishing bait.

Our friend Martha wrote that her grandfather smelled like "cigar tobacco, Aqua Velva, and Colgate toothpaste. Grandpa's earlobes and nostrils continued to grow long after the rest of him stopped.... He would eat onions and hot peppers straight from the garden, downing them with gusto and without tears, freeing me to do the same. He'd pull frosty bottles of Coca-Cola from the icebox, and vanilla ice cream from the deep freeze, and serve Coke floats and homemade popcorn balls for afternoon treats. All was right with the world."

Our friend Russell Cronkhite has written about such things in a more professional venue. Russell was executive chef at Blair House, the presidential guest home across the street from the White House. For twelve years he served three U.S. presidents and feasted their guests—kings, queens, prime ministers, presidents, and other heads of state from all over the world. Russell brings a redeemed Proustian understanding to the table. He knows that the sensory pleasures of the feast are a key to remembering our past and building memories for our children.

"Remember Sunday dinner?" Russell writes.

> Just hearing the words can take you back—perhaps to a well-loved dining room in your grandparents' house, where a stately oak table is laid with lace and hand-painted china. The table overflows with its Sunday bounty ... bowls of steaming, garden-fresh vegetables, crocks of sweet butter and homemade jam, and the succulent Sunday roast, juicy and brown. Incomparable aromas fill the house, laden with the promise of fresh-baked, light-as-a-feather biscuits or warm-from-the-oven peach cobbler.[2]

Even if our memories of Sunday dinner are not quite so idyllic, Russell's description touches a chord within. If it's not a remembrance of past feasts in a secure childhood home, then it's a sharp-sweet longing for a place of refuge. I find that I have an almost-tangible recall of things I never had. Though my childhood was warm and full, I often think of an imaginary grandmother's imaginary house. It has wrap-around porches, a Victorian turret, old-fashioned wallpaper with roses in the bedrooms, the smell of warm rolls in the big, bright kitchen. I believe these fake earthly memories are in fact intimations of and longings for the future, when I arrive in heaven and am Home for good.

At any rate, like Proust, I know that the nose is the gateway to the past.

Now of course the nose does not stand alone. The cheese stands alone, but not the nose. Other senses can also provide mysterious transport to the past, even in the most mundane settings . . . like the grocery store, for example. Our grocery is called Giant Food, which is a conundrum. Is Giant Food only for giants? Where do normal-sized people shop? Or is it giant food, like eggs the size of footballs and turkeys so large you can't close your oven door?

But I usually don't meditate on such things at my Giant. I just push my cart, the one with the squeaky wheel, up and down the stacked aisles. I am hoping I don't run into anyone I know because my brow is furrowed and my brain preoccupied. I am brooding about menus, vaguely wondering why I can't think of anything to cook for my family except grilled-cheese sandwiches. I am trying to remember what's already piled in my pantry. What happens, exactly, when canned goods expire? I am noting what's on sale and obediently putting these things in my cart, even if we don't like them, because it's buy one, get one free. And I am reflecting on the sheer repetition of it all. Why are my children hungry again? They ate yesterday. And the day before. I am thinking about the joys of eating out, and how my friend Ellie Lofaro says that when she calls to her kids that it's time for dinner, they all run to the car.

Then, in the Muzak that plays the perpetual soundtrack of modern life, I recognize a song. It is Van Morrison singing "Brown-Eyed Girl," which ruled pop radio thirty years ago. I'm still in the baked bean aisle, but the song transports me back to the summers of high school days, back to when I did not cook, back to when the warm green fields of my life stretched all the way to the blue horizon. The music plucks the chord of memory; it vibrates with a sweet-sharp sense of yearning, possibility, and melancholy. And it makes me grin, right there in the Giant.

Pachelbel's "Canon in D" does the same thing in a different way. The strong, sure strokes of its sweet strings waft me to my wedding day. When I hear bass voices singing "A Mighty Fortress," I move to the Mall between the Washington Monument and the United States Capitol, where I eavesdropped on a Promise Keeper's rally in 1997. My hair stood on end as a million men sang that hymn.

Neurologists say what these examples show: our senses lock in memories. The more senses that are involved, the more fully the memory is encoded in our brains. This is why any kid who's ever tried to memorize the books of the Bible can do so far more successfully if he or she sings them in a catchy tune. Memories involve both the limbic system, which carries emotional connections, as well as the cortex, with its visual, auditory, tactile, and olfactory centers. This is also why writers use metaphors, pastors use sermon illustrations, and the best speakers tell vivid stories. Abstract concepts like, say, the faithfulness of God remain abstract until they are locked into our minds through the senses.

So the Psalmist speaks of God as the caring shepherd of His sheep. Jesus told earthy earthly stories to convey heavenly meanings. And He picked up the Psalmist's trail, calling Himself the Good Shepherd who lays down His life for His flock. No mere metaphor: He lived and died it, the sacrificial Lamb of God, slain that His red blood might wash us white as snow.

When abstract concepts take on colors, tastes, smells, and emotional resonance, they bond with our minds in a new way. Even though we can't fully understand them, we can connect with them.

So my olfactory recall of my mother is not just a smell, but a tangible link to an intangible concept. Nina Ricci and sun-clean clothes are touchstones of my mom's love and God's faithfulness. Bus exhaust means the mountains of Colorado and sea salt means the ocean, but both are bigger than just those destinations. They connect me to the glories of God's great world.

God has designed us so that senses can serve as powerful Ebenezers of His faithfulness, and thereby be triggers of gratitude. This works even in the negative: I have a friend who rejoices whenever he happens to get a whiff of whiskey. The smell takes him, like an old smoke-filled cab, right to the dark alleys of his alcoholism. He feels again the horrors of slavery to all those Jim Beam bottles he felt compelled to empty. And he is flooded afresh with the joy of his deliverance. Even the odor of horrors past can point us to gratitude for God's gracious present.

But sensory perceptions are of course far more than links to times gone by. They are cause for profound pleasures today. I have found that the more I live in the fountain of God's grace, swimming in gratitude and splashing it back to Him, the more I revel in the sensory pleasures of everyday life. When we enjoy God's creation, we give glory to Him.

Along these lines, I love what John Piper says about C. S. Lewis.

> Lewis gave me an intense sense of the "realness" of things. The preciousness of this is hard to communicate. To wake up in the morning and be aware of the firmness of the mattress, the warmth of the sun's rays, the sound of the clock ticking, the sheer being of things ("quiddity" as he calls it). He helped me become alive to life. He helped me see what is there in the world—things that, if we didn't have, we would pay a million dollars to have, but having them, ignore. He made me more alive to beauty. He put my soul on notice that there are daily wonders that will waken worship if I open my eyes.[3]

Ah. The habit of giving thanks to God in all things opens our eyes to *daily wonders that will waken worship*. Gratitude is like a pair of glasses that get progressively sharper: the more I thank, the more I see to be thankful for, and the more I end up praising God.

This may sound simplistic, but it has had profound effects. I find that my senses are sharper. Food tastes better. Music makes me weep. I can take pleasure in a simple walk, without turning it into a tense strategic planning session about the next set of things that must get done. Gratitude unleashes the freedom to live content in the moment, rather than being anxious about the future or regretting the past. So one's focus is free to have not only a keener awareness of spiritual blessings, but the physical pleasures of everyday things we can taste, touch, hear, see, smell. The smell of fresh-cut grass. Shafts of sunlight piercing dark clouds. The perfection of my daughter's pearled ear. Wild geese that fly with the moon on their wings. The smell of fresh basil or popcorn or coffee in the mornings.

Scripture clearly differentiates between what is eternal and what is not. I do not lump the passing pleasure of my hot coffee with the lasting joy of my salvation. Nor, as we said in chapter 2, is the deepest sort of gratitude rooted in what God *gives*. It finds its source in *who God is*. But as we live in connection to Him, our reverent enthusiasm—regarding life's humblest details and its greatest joys—gives Him pleasure. All good gifts come from God. Not to enjoy them is to be ungrateful.

To paraphrase Abraham Kuyper's well-known quote about God's dominion over all things, there is not one aspect of our days, not one crispy potato chip crunched, nor one velvety rose inhaled, nor one dear friend hugged, heart to heart, over which God does not say "Mine." He is Lord.

Does this mean we slavishly chase every pleasure we can, glutting ourselves and rationalizing that it's all to the glory of God?

No. There is a difference between sensuality, which connotes self-indulgent preoccupation with fleshly appetites, and the sanctified enjoyment of sensory pleasures within God's good laws. What matters is what occupies our affections: the things themselves, or the One who gave them. Tactically, Satan takes good things and twists them. He would see us feebly snared in the senses rather than in bold love with their Creator. When we are occupied with the Giver, then we can hold His gifts with open hands, relishing them, but being at peace if they are taken away. To put it crassly, it's a win-win: we're not afraid to enjoy our stuff, and not afraid to lose it.

Psalm 115 compares those who worship God with those who worship other things. Idols are made by human hands, and they not only make no sense, they have no senses. They have mouths, but cannot speak, eyes, but they cannot see, the Psalmist says. They have ears that can't hear, noses that can't smell, hands that can't feel, and they cannot speak. And in the end, "Those who make them will be like them, and so will all who trust in them."[4]

I find this notion that we become just like our idols rather compelling. First, it explains why people who idolize their dogs start to look like them. Second, though few in North America actively worship totems of wood or stone, many focus their attention and affections on their wealth. They end up as unfeeling and incapable of real love as the cold bank vaults in which their financial documents and account numbers and stock transactions are stored.

Unlike such senseless idols, God is lavishly sensual. The Scriptures are full of descriptions of what He sees, smells, hears, feels, tastes . . . and He calls human beings to the feast as well. "Shout for joy to the LORD, . . . burst into jubilant song." "Taste and see that the LORD is good." "Come, all you who are thirsty, come to the waters . . . come, buy wine and milk without money and without cost." Jesus echoes, "Whoever drinks the water I give him will never thirst."[5]

In the Old Testament, when He is giving instructions about the design of His place of worship, God is in the sensory details. He gives specific directions about architecture, fabrics, colors, decorations, aromas by which human beings might be drawn to adore Him. God tells Moses to use cinnamon, olive oil, cassia . . . gold, silver, precious stones . . . linen, dyes, blue, purple, scarlet embroidery.

On a grander scale, creation itself reflects the glory of God. The world quivers with sensory beauty of every kind, just as His nature pulses with truth, beauty, joy. The Godhead rocks with love.

As a great friend of ours has said, a thankful heart gives a greater sensitivity to beauties both divine and mundane. He often finds himself sitting still in the moment and looking at what's around him, processing it all with different gradations of appreciation, but using the same word throughout: "Oh, Lord! I love my family. I love my house. I love the sky. I love this cup of coffee. I love You! Thank You!"

That's not only gratitude, and love, and worship. It's called joy.

Is this relegated to people who have a lot, and those who live in a shack or have scattered, broken families are shut out of the blessing?

No. In fact, I've learned the most about gratitude and worship and rich, overflowing joy, among people who have very little, in grim places that are poor indeed.

CHAPTER TWENTY-THREE

GARDEN
IN THE DUMP

The sovereign God wants to be loved for Himself and honored
for Himself, but that is only part of what He wants.
The other part is that He wants us to know that when we have
Him we have everything—we have all the rest.

A. W. Tozer

Years ago I had the pleasure of visiting Lurigancho, then one of the most notorious, violent, filthy, depraved prisons in the world.

I was part of a delegation of seven women; two of us were on staff with Prison Fellowship, and the rest were supporters of the ministry. We went to Peru and Ecuador to get a taste of Prison Fellowship's work in those nations.

In Peru, as we traveled by van from Lima's colorful city center, our hosts told us a little bit about Lurigancho. It had been built for about three thousand inmates; at the time of our visit it housed more than seven thousand. Murders, drug trafficking, and rape were common. A female television reporter and her crew had recently gone into the prison for a news story, and they had been attacked by inmates.

This did not increase our anticipation for our visit.

Neither did our surroundings as we approached the prison. We passed shantytowns on the edges of the city dumps; the air was heavy with the smells of garbage and human waste.

Then the paved road became dirt, the dirt became dust, and then it stopped: Lurigancho was the end of the road, a hellish fortress of ugly buildings in the dust. We wiped the sweat and dirt from our faces, climbed from the van, and were met at the enormous front gates by a small group of volunteers who go into that place all the time.

We passed through the black gates. The stench was overwhelming, a dense mixture of the odors of unwashed bodies, overripe meat cooking in open pots, pools of urine in the corridors, and the stink of open sewers.

We were taken to the office of the prison superintendent. An immense man with a thick, black mustache, he was wearing a dirty undershirt, green fatigues, and army boots. He was sitting at a small metal desk, pecking with two fingers on an ancient manual typewriter. A large poster of a naked woman hung on his office wall.

We were then cleared, if that is the right word, to pass into the interior of the prison, to a special wing where inmates who had become followers of Jesus were all housed in one section. We passed through another dark, odorous corridor and a series of doors and gates ... and then we were in the Christian sector.

I could not believe the disparity between this oasis and the rest of the prison. The walls and floors were clean, the only posters were pictures of Jesus, and the inmates' faces shone as well. They smiled, bowed, shook our hands, made us welcome.

We were introduced to the men by Sister Anna, an American nun who had worked in Lurigancho for twenty years. She was from Detroit, a small, quick woman with a matter-of-fact manner and a big grin. She took us through the wing, smiling, shouting to inmates, clapping others on the back. "These fellas are the greatest," she said. "Let me show you what they've done outside."

"Outside" was a walled courtyard area in the center of Lurigancho. Open to the sky, it had once been an exercise area but had become too dangerous. So for years, everyone in the prison had used it as a garbage dump and cesspool. Then, inspired, Sister Anna asked the warden if the Christian community could have the dump. He had shrugged, laughed, and given it to her to manage.

Now, leading us, Sister Anna opened a big wooden door in the cell-block wall. The inmates stood aside to let us go first. We passed through the door . . . and I saw huge, vibrant pink hibiscus, red geraniums, clusters of purple and yellow blooms. I saw enormous sunflowers, their faces turned toward the sky above the prison walls. I saw trailing vines swaying in the breeze, a long, well-tended rectangle of tender, green grass, a fountain of fresh water flowing in the center . . . and around the corner, neat rows of young vegetables.

After God had cleaned up their lives, the Christian inmates had cleaned up the dung heap—and now it was a lovely garden, overflowing with fruits and flowers.

Later, I talked with a man named Roberto. He was in his late thirties, with dark hair and steady green eyes. An attorney who spoke English, he had been a person of some means. But because of money-laundering in his company, here he was at the end of the road in Lurigancho. He laughed as he told me how he slept on the concrete floor, since there was only one cot and his cell mate needed it more than he did. It was a far cry from corporate life.

But for Roberto, Lurigancho was not the end. It was the beginning. "Coming here is the best thing that ever happened to me," he said. "I found Jesus here. I have another year on my sentence, but I don't want to go out. I want others to know that there *is* hope, even in a place like this. Before I was always chasing after the next thing. Now I am clear inside. I want them to know that they can change, like I changed, through the power of God."

Later we visited several women's prisons. In one dilapidated institution, we worshipped God with the inmates in their chapel.

The women sang, shared poetry they had written, and performed an interpretation of the Prodigal Son parable, complete with pigs.

Just before we had to leave, these prodigal women closed the chapel doors. They turned out the lights. Then they passed slim white candles, lighting them one by one as we stood in a circle. They sang a final hymn, the flames lighting the soft darkness, their voices blending in harmony. This was not a performance for the North American guests. One woman sang with tears coursing down her cheeks, her face turned up toward heaven, her candle burning steadily. She was singing to her Lord.

Afterward, I walked out onto the dry pavement in the hot prison courtyard, and this woman followed me. She had shining, dark hair, high cheekbones, and a big smile. In careful English, she said slowly, "I ... love ... you!" She paused, working on her next words. "We are ... SISTERS!" Then she hugged me hard.

In another women's prison, I went into a cell that was barely bigger than the bunk bed in it. A woman was lying in the lower bunk under a ragged blanket; her cell mate pulled the blanket back, and there was a tiny infant in the bed with her. "*Tiene ocho semanas*," she said. Eight weeks old.

There were lots of children like this: infants, toddlers, kids playing with an old soccer ball in the prison courtyard. Many had never been outside the prison walls in their lives. There is no place else for them to go.

It was just after Christmas, and we distributed gifts for the children, in Jesus' name. They jumped up and down as we handed out the packages. I watched one little girl as she carefully loosed the bright paper on her box. She pulled off the lid, and her eyes widened. Inside was a soft doll with long, curling hair. She pulled the doll out of the package and cradled her gently next to her heart.

Later, when we had to leave, I looked back to the prison entrance to lock a final image in my mind. I saw that small child and her mother. They were smiling, calling out their thanks, and waving good-bye. And about fifteen feet above them, walking the perimeter of that prison compound, was a uniformed guard cradling a submachine gun.

A child holding her doll as her mother holds her close, even as the armed guard patrols their prison wall. The soft hug of a sister behind iron bars. Men in Lurigancho's black hole planting a bright garden. These believers I met in South America were poor, by earthly standards. They were in terrible places, by any standard. And yes, they needed help from those of us who have been so materially blessed.

But when I think of those pictures from prison, what I remember most is these friends' rich joy and worship, their urgent desire that others might know the hope they've known. What they had in common was uncommon: grateful hearts. And in that, I can learn from them.

CHAPTER TWENTY-FOUR

GO!

If we ourselves have known anything of the love of Christ for us,
and if our hearts have felt any measure of gratitude
for the grace that has saved us from death and hell,
then this attitude of compassion and care
for our spiritually needy fellow-men ought
to come naturally and spontaneously to us....

It is a tragic and ugly thing when Christians lack desire,
and are actually reluctant, to share the precious knowledge
that they have with others whose need of it
is just as great as their own.

J. I. Packer

Having heartily pumped the pleasures of life's daily blessings
in chapter 22, am I now saying that we should chuck them all
to go live among the poor?

Certainly, if we're called to do so.

But even if we are not specifically led to sell all and live with
people in poverty, we still must weave our lives with theirs. For
even as we relish our temporal blessings, we hold these goods with
open hands. We're not in love with the stuff, but with its Creator.
This means we are free. Free to enjoy God's gifts, free to share
them, free to come, and free to go. We don't make a nest and

perpetually rest in the soft cushions of our comforts. We leave them and *go* to those who are uncomfortable.

We go for several reasons.

We go because Jesus commissioned His followers to go everywhere carrying the good Gospel news.[1] Christ had no intention for His people to stay in our cozy shells like clams. As we are going about our ordinary business, and as we go to odd places He calls us, we irrepressibly bear witness to Him. There are no "proper" itineraries that we all must follow to the letter of the law in order to be considered "good" Christians. Each of us will come and go according to the Spirit's quiet call within. We must listen for it.

We go, also, because of the authority of the One who commissions us, the One who was tortured and executed in our place. Those who are filled with thankfulness for so great a deliverance are happy indeed to go. Wherever. Whenever.

Thus we report to Him for duty. *Where to, Sir? Here I am. Send me!*

We go as well because Jesus said in serving those who are poor and needy, we are serving Him. And we go because we can learn far more about Christ's sufficiency for our real needs, and about real thankfulness, from the believing poor than from the comfortable rich. Going increases our own gratitude.

Now, the poor are not inherently noble by virtue of their poverty. Those who have little can be as miserly, selfish, and prideful as those who have a lot. Sin and grace both cut across economic lines, for they are centered in the human heart.

But the poor do have an advantage, as Jesus pointed out in the Sermon on the Mount. Because they have little in this world, they are less likely to be distracted from the Kingdom of God or taken in by illusions of self-sufficiency. It is one thing to pray for your daily bread when your pantry and wallet are full, and so is the gourmet store down the street. It is another to pray for bread when, like some of our brothers in Cuba, your ration for the month is gone, you have no money, and the stores are empty anyway. You have to trust in God alone.

When we go, it needn't be to some faraway destination. God might send us to a soup kitchen, homeless shelter, hospice, or housing project. We don't have to get a passport and head for a prison in Peru.

In fact, based on my experience, you probably should not go to prisons in Peru unless you are a good dancer.

In one institution I visited, our little delegation of women was escorted to the front of the cell block. There were about 150 inmates, no guards, some Prison Fellowship Peru volunteers, and us. The inmates recited poetry they had written and told how they had found Jesus in prison. They presented each of us with a red rose. Then they kicked off the musical portion of the program. One man played a flute, another a guitar, a third a leather drum. The tune was lilting, insistent, infectious. It was a lot like Irish folk music, but completely different.

I sat on a wooden chair, tapping my foot and smiling big. Then came the surprise. An inmate approached me, his arms outstretched, his palms and eyebrows up. In spite of the language barrier, it was clear he was inviting me to dance.

My stomach turned with an odd feeling I had not experienced since the seventh-grade mixer. I did not want to dance just then. I tried to figure out how to gracefully decline.

But then, as always, the great question came into my mind: *What would Jesus do?*

Up I leapt. Jesus would dance in prison. I think.

The problem was, I'm sure Jesus is a better dancer than me. I couldn't quite figure out just what we were supposed to be doing. My inmate grabbed my waist and we whirled around in some odd combination of North Carolina beach shagging and Peruvian boogie. My partner was quite gallant, flinging me this way and that; the crowd of prisoners was cheering, whistling, and shouting in Spanish. In the din I dimly realized that other inmates had pulled my friends into the mix. Maria, our translator, was Peruvian, so she was doing fine. And out of the corner of one eye I saw my colleague Alma flinging by on the arm of her inmate in some South American version of the Virginia Reel.

In the midst of this shindig my brain and I were having one of those split-screen conversations that click in now and then.

"And where are you now?" my brain asked politely.

"Well, I'm in prison in South America," I said.

"Oh?" said my brain. "And what are you doing?"

"Just dancing with the inmates!" I responded cheerily.

"Splendid, splendid," my brain said in a charming British accent, sounding just like the distracted father in *Mary Poppins*.

Then, mercifully, the inmate band came to the end of their set. I returned to my seat, filled with a new and deeper meaning of the term "fool for Christ."

Several years after my prison jamboree, a writing project took me out of the U.S. every few months. So when my brain would ask just where I was, I'd report that I was wading in the South China Sea, or worshipping with believers in Havana, and or staring out an airplane window at the distant peak of Mount Everest.

One week I'd be bumping along in the back of a muddy oxcart in the Cambodian jungle, trying to take notes as I interviewed a scarred survivor of Pol Pot's killing fields. The next week I'd be navigating our Chevy Suburban in the carpool line at school, eyes crossing as I listened to the kids strapped in the back seats playing "Hot Cross Buns" on their recorders. Over and over. One Sunday I'd be dancing (badly, of course) with a converted former witch-doctor in a village in India, then sharing cups of weak tea and warm bread ... the next I'd be reciting the Nicene Creed in my suburban Washington church, a congressman in the next pew and an ambassador across the aisle, then out to brunch with friends.

During this time, one morning I found myself on the coast of India at dawn, on the Bay of Bengal. A lighthouse flashed as the dark receded and the day began. Birds called to one another. The fishermen were returning with their night's catch, their narrow boats pulling up on the shore. A group of women approached in flowing saris, tall woven baskets balanced on their heads. They filled them with fresh fish for the morning's market. As I watched, thinking we all might as well be in Jesus' time, I heard unusual sounds on the sand behind me. I turned around.

It was a small herd of cows.

I had no previous experience with cows on the beach. My mind scrambled desperately to reconcile two images with which it was familiar—yes, I had seen cows and I had been on many a beach— but had never before perceived simultaneously. I felt like I had stepped into a Salvador Dali painting. No melting clocks, just bovines by the seaside, and a cow is a humorous thing to begin with.

At any rate, the juxtapositions of surreal international adventures and my usual domestic life opened my eyes, more and more, to the daily blessings that are so easy to take for granted. They filled me with gratitude, which welled up in a reservoir of thankfulness that sustained me, and grew even greater, in the aftermath of my mother's death a year or so afterwards.

I've experienced other lasting take-aways from those travels. For one, I no longer take indoor plumbing lightly. I revel in clean, hot water, and fragrant soap in my morning shower. I'm amazed by soft carpet under my bare feet. At the grocery, I can barely contain my exhilaration at the overwhelming abundance: sleek, bright vegetables, fresh herbs, fat cheeses, every kind of meat and milk and bread and wine.

And again, I think of the believers I've met abroad who have so little ... yet their energy and joy are enormous.

Meanwhile, in the first world, television and magazines profile the lifestyles of the super rich, as if they are the standard by which we should all assess our own material existence. Accordingly, many average Americans—even though they enjoy a lifestyle better than 99.4 percent of all the human beings who have ever lived[2]—strain for more.

In an acquisitive, consumer culture there is no such thing as enough, for contented people don't buy more. Advertising and marketing fan the flames of discontent and covetousness. So there is always the newest fashion, the latest model, the next upgrade that everyone else has . . . gotta have it. So people buy more—and are satisfied less.

Griping rises with income, concluded two economists who studied the U.S. and four other wealthy nations. "People who were otherwise statistically similar (same age, working hours, number of children) complained more about the 'time squeeze' as their incomes rose."[3] The economists concluded that "the more money people have, the more things they can do with their time; time becomes more valuable, and people increasingly resent that they can't create more of it."[4]

Similarly, *The Paradox of Choice: Why More is Less* cites that consumers can compare between "220 new car models, 250 breakfast cereals, 400 VCRs, 40 household soaps, 500 health insurance policies, 350 mutual funds, and even 35 showerheads."[5] People feel overwhelmed by the burden of having to research the best option. After they buy, if they feel they made the wrong choice, then they're miserable.

Gregg Easterbrook's well-received book *The Progress Paradox: How Life Gets Better While People Feel Worse*,[6] cites the amazing rise in Americans' standard of living. But here's the paradox: in the same period that people's material lives have improved dramatically, their inner lives have declined: depression, loneliness, and frustration are all much higher than they were fifty years ago.

Easterbrook's prescription? Put generally, he says that we need to stop focusing on ourselves and instead concentrate on being grateful for our daily blessings, on the deeper truths of what really matters in life, and on what we can do to help our neighbors around the world.

This is why going to places that are uncomfortable, among people in real need, is a great antidote to the complacency and complaints that so easily creep into a consuming lifestyle.

Our friends Jerry and Holly are go-ers.

Some years ago Jerry was in Russia on a short visit with Prison Fellowship International. He and a group of friends visited a number of prisons, and finished their work a few days early. They asked their hosts if they could go visit children in the hospital.

They were taken to a 750-bed hospital in Moscow at the end of the Leninski Prospect. Most of the beds were empty. This is where children with cancer and blood diseases came to die. There was a cafeteria but no food. No trained nurses, no laundry, no disinfectants, few medicines, no lab work. The children's families brought in and prepared food for them in the empty hospital kitchen.

This was the national clinic for children, where patients came from all over the Russian Federation.

A staff person brought a young girl in an old wheelchair to Jerry. She was about fourteen years old, with thin brown hair and dark circles under her eyes. "She has about four months to live," the woman told Jerry. "We have no medicines to help her."

"What is her name?" Jerry asked. He bent down to the girl's level.

"Eugenia," the woman said.

Jerry rocked on his heels. Eugenia was his daughter's name. What if *his* Eugenia was dying and needed medicine? What would he do? What would this Russian Eugenia's dad do for his daughter, if he could?

The staff people told Jerry that the drug protocol for Eugenia would run about $18,000 U.S. Jerry is not a man of wealth, but he turned to a buddy with him, a cattle rancher. "Ed," said Jerry, "if we can't find someone to donate the money to help this little girl, I'll sell my car, if you sell your truck, okay?"

"You drive me crazy always trying to swing these deals," Ed said. "But that's why I come on these trips with you. Okay."

But selling a car and a truck would only take them so far. There were lots of kids who needed help.

Jerry returned to the U.S. and got on the phone. Within two weeks, a prominent children's clinic had given him tens of thousands of dollars' worth of drugs packed in cooler boxes with dry ice, and Jerry was on a plane back to Moscow.

When he and his buddies walked into the hospital in the night, Eugenia's mother saw them coming. She ran down the dim corridor, her face incredulous, and burst into tears. "You are Jesus, are you not?" she exclaimed in broken English.

As he puts it, Jerry explained to her that they were very unaccomplished followers of Jesus, who had told them to help Eugenia and bring some medicine. Aside from that, Jerry told the Russian mother, they didn't know all that much.

Eugenia went through the protocol and into remission. After that a foundation run by Jerry's friends David and Catherine Bradley partnered with the clinic with the goal to turn it from a hospice into a hospital. Then the Gorbachev Foundation gave a $2 million bone marrow transplant unit. Many other companies came alongside, donating everything from medicines to blood filters to medical supplies.

Now that clinic is world class. It is the best place in Russia to be treated for pediatric blood diseases. Now there are chapel services for kids and their families, run by a little band of Russian believers. David and Catherine Bradley paid for a certified teaching nurse to go to Russia for two years to work with and train the Russian nurses. And Russian doctors from the clinic go out around the Federation, training less-educated country doctors.

Now, says Jerry, "we have worked our way out of a job, and hardly anyone at the clinic would know who we are. But that was the plan all along, to go, do it quietly, and then disappear."

I tell Jerry's story not to blow his cover, but because it's such a great model of how God can use His people when they go. His activism changed the lives of kids on the other side of the world.

When another friend obeyed God's call to "go," it was just across the street, to someone who was materially well-to-do but spiritually quite needy.

Caroline had developed a friendship with a woman in her upscale Florida development. Her neighbor was as skittish as a fawn. But gradually, as Fawn began to trust her, Caroline discovered that her husband was addicted to Internet pornography, that her teenaged sons were caught in the same trap, and their house was full of rage, fear, lust, and shame.

Late one night police cars shrieked into the neighborhood and into Fawn's driveway. Caroline could see other neighbors who'd been awakened, peeking through their drapes and looking out their front doors as it became apparent that there had been some sort of altercation. But no one was going to Fawn's door to help.

"I'm going," Caroline told her husband. She went across the street and asked what she could do. She hugged her neighbor, talked like a tough aunt to the teenaged boys, one of whom had attacked the other, answered some of the police officers' questions, and made everyone a big pot of tea. No miracles occurred—that evening, anyway. But Caroline was right where God called her to go.

Going means giving up my own beloved agenda in favor of something much bigger and better. For example, once I was having a dinner party, and as I ran around making preparations, I kept thinking about a neighbor. I'll call her Carla, which is appropriate, since that is her name.

Carla was a loving, funny, generous friend. As we had spent time together, she had opened up more and more. She had a lot of questions about her past and uncertainties about her future. Coming from a works-and-guilt-oriented background, it was hard for her to fathom the free gift of God's grace.

Now, this particular afternoon, I couldn't get Carla off my mind. Meanwhile I had cuisine to cook and candles to light and corners to clean. Going to Carla's house was not on my to-do list.

But in the end, even I could tell that I had to go.

I dropped in. She was alone, which was unusual. We sat on her white sofa. I asked her if she was ready to receive Christ.

She was. She did.

And I was quite glad that I went.

Going needn't stop as we age, if health allows.

John Piper writes about a couple who retired and spent their days cruising on their thirty-foot trawler and collecting shells. Piper bemoans the mixed-up priorities and missed opportunities. "Picture them before Christ at the great day of judgment," he says. " 'Look, Lord. See my shells.' "

With that in mind, I respect the way my dad used his golden years to go to others.

Chuck Colson always said that my dad looked like he had come straight out of Central Casting, and Chuck was right. Carl Santilli was a short, round man with bright, dark eyes, black, military issue glasses, and a big nose with a gray mustache beneath it. A retired Army colonel, he wore the last twelve hairs that remained on his head squared off on top. He whistled most places he went.

Dad came to Christ when he was in his midfifties. (This, in spite of G. K. Chesterton's observation that "a change of opinions is almost unknown in an [older] military man."[7]) Dad lived the remaining twenty-five years of his life with a great sense of urgency, as if he was making up for lost time. He studied the Bible with fervor, taught Sunday School, helped people in need. He went into the county jail to lead a Bible study once a week. He gave ex-offenders a hand whenever he could. He even attempted to teach the Bible to my certifiably crazy Aunt Cecelia, who lived in a broken-down house in Washington with twenty-seven cats.

(Aunt Cecelia had been in a near-fatal car wreck years earlier in which she had irretrievably lost part of her brain. After she was released from the hospital she went to work for the Internal Revenue Service for many years, but that's another story.)

At any rate, I remember one time near the end of his life when Dad attended a reunion of old military buddies. These men—the "greatest generation" who had served in World War II—reminisced about their sealed orders after Pearl Harbor, their battles, their buddies who didn't come home.

Then the conversation shifted to how they spent their time in retirement. Things lagged a bit; it seemed many of them got a good deal more energy from remembering the past. They listened politely while Dad told them about his Bible study in the jail. But most of the rest of the evening, it seemed, revolved around old war stories and one man's hobby, which he recounted in great detail: making his own corned beef.

Later, Dad told me how frustrated he'd felt, how superficial it had seemed to him. "Here the world out there is going to hell," he said, "and all these guys can talk about is the right way to make corned beef!"

Dad was not without his warts. But he was a person whose gratitude to God for his own rescue overflowed in the desire to help others.

Again, as with my dad's ministry at the local jail, we need not go far. But there is something fresh and bracing about getting out of town.

Lee and I started taking our kids on summer missions trips when the twins were eight and Emily eleven. The first year we went to the Cherokee Nation in the mountains of North Carolina. At night we slept in little cabins on the reservation, ate in a mess hall, mopped floors, and poked campfires with long, smoking sticks. The stars were glorious. Walker, Haley, and Emily ran through the mountain trails just like Daniel Day-Lewis in the opening scenes of the film version of *Last of the Mohicans*.

Our family, and others from our church, went to a nursing home and sang hymns with the ancient residents. Each morning we went to a senior center on the reservation and visited with elderly widows. We heard their life stories of domestic violence, alcoholism, poverty, the deaths of children, spouses, and loved ones. We learned about strength and dignity in terrible situations. I watched Emily develop a friendship with a beautiful Cherokee grandmother named Mrs. Reed. I loved watching them walk slowly down the halls, holding hands.

At midday we would leave our older friends and take a picnic lunch of squashed peanut butter sandwiches to our team members who were building a deck for a Cherokee widow. Then we'd careen to a day-care center run by the reservation, which gives Christian groups permission to come in and run mini Bible-school camps.

The kids were bouncing off the walls. They were affectionate, outspoken, and had rather brief attention spans. They were kept in order by a huge, attentive, and slightly scary Indian named Buck Squirrel, who gave me permission to write that.

We let the kids spray shaving cream and throw water balloons on the playground. We told Bible stories with all our might. We served them snacks to illustrate the stories. A graham cracker with peanut butter and a thin, apple-slice sail was Jonah's boat. A hamburger bun with a marshmallow inside was the pearl of great price. We told the kids how Jesus said that God's love is like a fine pearl, or a hidden treasure. It's so amazing and beautiful that when you find it, He becomes the most important thing in your life.

Emily had celebrated her birthday just before we came to Cherokee, and Lee's mother had given her a necklace. It was a silver chain with a filigree pendant. The pendant had a small catch and could open and close. Nestled inside was a creamy, perfect pearl.

One day, under the supervision of our fearless leader, Mr. Ed, Emily was using the nail gun at the construction site. It kicked back powerfully against her each time she released it and slammed a three-inch nail into the wood.

It wasn't until a day later that Emily realized her necklace was gone. We looked everywhere. Walker kindly scooched in the crawl space underneath the low deck and found the necklace. But the catch had popped open, and there was no pearl.

On the last day of our trip, we held an impromptu dedication service with the homeowner on her new deck. We prayed for her, and thanked God for our time in Cherokee.

Emily nudged me after the prayer. "Mom," she said. "I wanted to pray about my pearl, but it seemed selfish." I nodded and hugged her shoulders. Then we all posed on the new deck for a group photo. As soon as the picture was taken, Emily looked straight down, bent to the deck, and picked something up. It was her pearl.

Does God ensure that a young girl will find her pearl? Sometimes. Sometimes not. But I do know that if we will go, and look, and bend, He hides gifts to be discovered, right in the sawdust of life.

That first family missions trip to Cherokee was certainly not hard labor. It was a way to get our children started, to dip their toes in the swift rivers of God's big world, so splendidly full of people and opportunities.

On our afternoon off, we went tubing on a nearby river. We rented big inner tubes that looked like enormous black doughnuts with handles. Wearing our bathing suits and old tennis shoes, we rolled them a mile up the path through the woods next to the river. It was just like rolling tires, which I guess makes sense. It was June, and the river was raw and swollen with swift waters rushing down from the mountains. It had only just slightly thawed from a frozen state.

Now, I should explain that I am a weenie when it comes to cold water. There are other things I can brave, like snakes and heights and dark alleys in foreign lands, but at home I won't even go into our neighborhood swimming pool until it's the proper temperature to poach fish. My morning shower steams the mirror. I love hot water.

But this Cherokee river water, tumbling down the rapids, was liquid ice. I put my foot into the shallowest part near the shore and my brain shut down. There was no way I was going to do this.

Meanwhile Lee and the children, who have some important temperature regulator missing from their body chemistry, waded right in. They settled their tubes and plopped themselves in. The current began to carry them toward the first set of rapids.

The choice: I could stay warm and dry and sit out the adventure. Or I could be quite uncomfortable and let the river take me where it willed.

The others were floating away. I could hear laughing and yelling from just around the bend. They were calling for me.

It was not going to get any easier. My body just had to act, rather than wait for my brain to come to terms with this decision.

I waded in. My feet, then my legs went numb. In the shallows, I steadied the tube beneath me and hopped miserably onto it, arms and legs clutching the sides like a desperate spider, my rear end dragging as little as possible in the icy water. In a moment I was swept into the first set of rapids. Screaming, I arched my back as high as I could without losing balance and upending my tube. Cruel people I didn't even know, watching from the shore, laughed out loud.

I caught up with my family. The river took us all the way downstream. It was wonderful.

Go.

CHAPTER TWENTY-FIVE

THE REST OF THE STORY: EXTRAVAGANT GRATITUDE

All we deserve from God is judgment. . . . Therefore every breath we take,
every time our heart beats, every day that the sun rises,
every moment we see with our eyes or hear with our ears or speak
with our mouths or walk with our legs is, for now, a free and
undeserved gift to sinners who deserve only judgment.

I say "for now" because if you refuse to see God in His gifts, they will
turn out not to be gifts but High Court evidence of ingratitude. . . .

But for those who see the merciful hand of God in every breath
they take and give credit where it is due, Jesus Christ will be seen
and savored as the great Purchaser of every undeserved breath.
Every heartbeat will be received as a gift from His hand.

John Piper, *Don't Waste Your Life*

Once Jesus was invited to dinner at a religious leader's home. In the Eastern style of the day, He was reclining at the low table, His bare feet stretched out behind Him.

A woman with a bad reputation crept into the home. She slipped behind Jesus and knelt. Sobbing, she covered His feet with her tears, then wiped them dry with her long, unbound hair. She broke open an alabaster jar of priceless perfume and smoothed the rich ointment on Jesus' heels. The perfume filled the house.

Disgusted, the pharisaical host sniffed to himself that Jesus must not be much of a prophet if He didn't know what kind of woman was embracing His feet.

Jesus was enough of a prophet to know exactly what the man was thinking. He told him a little story.

Two men owed money to a lender. One owed five hundred, the other fifty. Neither could pay him back, and the lender canceled both debts. Which man loved him more?

"I suppose the one who had the greater debt canceled," said the Pharisee, grudgingly.

Correct, said Jesus.[1]

Sometimes, like the Pharisee, we can shy away from the sinful woman's display. It's so, uh, *physical*. So intimate. So extravagant.

Jesus knew her by name. He knew the broken shards of her sins, her shame. And He forgave her. Extravagantly.

This woman loved much, her grateful, repentant tears like a fountain, for she was forgiven much. As Jesus said, the connection is clear: if we think we've only been forgiven a little, we'll only have a little love, a little joy, a little gratitude. We might be materially rich ... but we'll be spiritual paupers. Only those who know the woeful depths of their sin can intuitively praise God for the luxurious heights of His grace.

The extent to which we truly love is connected to the degree that we are stunned and silenced by "the wonder that [our] huge debt has been canceled," says Dan Allender. "... A stunned and grateful heart is free to love because it has been captured with the hilarious paradox that we are unlovely but loved, and unable to love but free to try without condemnation."[2]

There is another point that flows out of this, an extravagantly difficult one. Those who know they are truly, deeply forgiven are able to do what is otherwise impossible. Figuring that the enormity of their own debt has been canceled, they are free to cancel the debts of those who have sinned against them. They forgive others.

I have a dear friend who can speak to this. I'll call her Jane, for it is important to change a few identifying details about her story. But it is true.

It was a week before Christmas, 1974. Jane Jones was twenty-five years old, beautiful, talented, full of enthusiasm, energy, and exuberance. She and her husband, Daniel, had been married for five years. He was an attorney, and Jane had her own daily television talk show in the capitol city of a Midwestern state. Jane would get up each weekday morning at 6:00, gulp some coffee, kiss her husband good-bye, and head for the TV studio, an hour's drive away. She'd arrive in time to go over her interview questions, meet with her guests, and get settled before the cameras rolled at 9:00 a.m.

Since her audience was primarily female, Jane focused on subjects that were relevant to women's lives. A week earlier she had aired a show on sexual assault. At the time—an era long before Oprah—such issues weren't commonly discussed on television, particularly in conservative markets. But Jane felt that a program on this taboo topic could help women who'd been violated and felt afraid, ashamed, alone. Her producer agreed.

The show featured two guests who had been raped. Their faces were shadowed, identities hidden. Jane gently questioned them about their experiences and the aftermath of the crimes. A police officer and a district attorney were guests as well.

Afterward, the studio was flooded with calls and mail. Jane wept as she read the letters from women who had been so grateful for the show. So many victims . . . so much pain.

Now, a week later, Jane was going to stay in town for several days to tape a few programs. Her parents and brother were coming for Christmas, and she wanted to get some shows in the can so she could take time off to be with them. She checked into the hotel across the street from the television studio.

At about 10:00 that evening, she was sitting at the desk in her room, working on the next day's scripts. She was sleepy, but still had work to do . . . so she took her key, went downstairs to the hotel restaurant, and got a cup of coffee. She came back to the room, unlocked the door, and returned to the desk. She stretched for a moment, then sat down, her back to the curtained windows.

A moment later the curtains parted, and in a flash the man who'd been hiding there grabbed Jane from behind. She felt the cold steel of a gun muzzle on her temple and his heavy, gloved hand around her neck. He bent down and hissed in her ear. "Okay, Miss Cute Little Talk Show Host. What do you do with a gun to your head?"

He dragged her to the bed. She fought with all her strength. She struggled, pled, and prayed as he held her in a vicious stranglehold and raped her over and over and over again. He had a ski mask pulled over his face; all she knew was that he was tall, black, muscular, strong. He taunted her, always with the gun in one hand, much of the time with it pressed against her head. "I will kill you if you tell," he spat at her. "I know where you live."

"I can't live through this," Jane cried out to God. "I won't live through this."

An hour went by, and more. He pushed her down. Pointing the gun at her head, he backed slowly away, then turned and climbed out the window. The roof of the parking garage was just below. Jane heard him drop onto it and slip away into the night.

Jane's clothes were torn, her body ripped. She felt filthy, violated, and overwhelmed by a fear as deadly as that cold gun barrel. She called the police, the hotel front desk, her husband. "I've been raped," she sobbed to Daniel on the phone. "I need you. Please come and hold me." Then she huddled in a chair, wept, and waited.

The police arrived. A female officer questioned Jane, making her repeat every detail of the assault. They took her to the hospital emergency room, and then the police station. She felt Jesus give her the strength to somehow repeat it again and again. Daniel arrived; he had been two hours away at his parents' home. He held her gently, swallowing his own roiling rage, murmuring to her over and over like a child, "I love you. It's going to be all right."

The next morning Jane called the manager of the TV station and told him what had happened. "I've got to appear on the show this morning," she said, her heart pounding. "Otherwise he'll know I told. I know he'll be watching." She felt like a robot. She somehow did the show. Meanwhile the police—and her husband—were doing everything they could to pursue her attacker. Aside from the physical markers he'd left in Jane, there were no leads. "He's done this before," Jane told the police. "He was a professional. You've got to find him. He'll do it to somebody else."

When she finally got home later that day, Jane went to bed. Her doctor had given her medicine to help her sleep. Her bruises ached, her body was raw. And her heart was broken. She had always been a trusting, open, affectionate person. Something inside that had been shiny and trusting was gouged and crushed. The rapist's sadism had stolen her joy. His rage had filled her with fear. Even though it made no sense, his hatred made her feel guilty. *It was my fault*, she thought, even though it made no sense. *After all, I did that show on rape.* She curled in her bed, weeping.

The next day, Jane's parents and brother arrived for the Christmas holidays. Jane was determined not to tell them what had happened; she wanted to protect them from the horror. Her public persona took over, and she stuffed the pain and fear down deep inside. She hosted a long-planned party for a hundred guests. Over the holiday she laughed, toasted, gave lovely gifts. At night she shook and wept as her husband held her close and wept as well.

On the Monday after Christmas, it was time to return to the television studio. Jane got up, put on her makeup, drank coffee, chatted with her brother as she got ready to go . . . and then suddenly she was overwhelmed by terror: the drenching fear of the cold gun at her temple, the thick fingers gripping her neck . . . she passed out in a heap on the floor.

When Jane came to, her brother's arms were around her. Her parents were with them, and Daniel was leaning over her. "It's all right," he said gently. "I've told them what happened. You don't need to hide it any more."

But soon a new fear arose. Her period did not come. One month. Two. Three. Every few weeks Jane returned to her gynecologist. "It's stress," he told her. "Really. Please don't worry."

Somehow Jane returned to her daily show. She did all the energetic things she used to do, on autopilot. But on her commute home in the evenings, tapes from the night of fear would play in her mind. She'd stop at an old bridge not far from her home, turn off the ignition, and weep and cry out to God. Then she'd put her face back on and drive home. Perky, fun Jane, just like always.

Finally, her period did come. She was not pregnant—except with fear and shame. Her pain was a dense, growing mass inside. "I know where you live," her attacker said again and again in her mind. She could hear his voice, feel the gun's cold muzzle, hear his taunts. "I will kill you if you tell."

Months went by. She quit her television show and got another job. The police reported in occasionally: no trace of the rapist. In his wake, Jane found that part of her was normal, able to love her husband and live her life. But part of her was dying inside.

Then Daniel, a golden man who'd always had political ambitions, decided to run for public office. Campaigning would mean crisscrossing the state, media coverage, newspaper stories about them both. Jane knew Daniel could serve the people well. Her "life as normal" side was ready to jump right into the political race and cheer her husband on. But at the same time her fears were coiled inside, always ready to strike.

She called her closest friend, who lived in another state. "Can you come?" she sobbed into the phone. Her friend Pat quit her job, left her house, and joined Jane and Daniel on the campaign trail. It reminded Jane of what she had read about African elephants. When one is wounded, if it falls to the ground it will die. So two other elephants will come next to the wounded one, one on each side, and bear its great weight until it is healed. Daniel and Pat were her elephants.

That thought helped her. Then something else happened, something quite odd but wonderful. Her feet began to smell. They nauseated her. She mentioned it to her mother on the phone. "You're pregnant!" her mom told her. "When I was pregnant, I just could not get my feet far enough away from my nose!"

Propelled by this strange revelation, Jane returned to her gynecologist. Her mom was right. She felt a small flame of the joy that used to be her constant companion but had been robbed by her attacker. She thought about her fears right after the rape ... but now she was having a child by Daniel. What could have been a child of shame was instead a child of love.

Daniel was elected. They moved to Washington, DC. Jane was nine months and three weeks pregnant. And during the president's State of the Union address in January, she went into labor on the floor of the United States Congress. The baby waited until she and Daniel got to the hospital. With the birth of their daughter, joy once again filled their lives.

Life was busy but sweet. Jane and Daniel made new friends whose faith went deep. Their roots spread and took hold more firmly in God's love and grace.

Then came the day when baby Mollie was about four months old. Carrying her, Jane walked up the front steps to their home after being out one afternoon. There were splinters of wood on the step. The door had been jammed. Jane pushed it open, and everything was turned upside down. Her heart jerked; she vaguely noticed that the television and VCR were gone.

On autopilot, illogically, she carried Mollie to her room and gently tucked her in her crib. "I don't want her to be afraid," she thought. "I don't want her to see me fall apart." She carefully shut Mollie's door, then came back to the living room and fell on the hardwood floor, facedown. "God!" she cried. "I cannot live with this again. You've got to save me from this fear. I don't want to be a victim! I need you!"

She had never experienced anything like what happened next. A warm covering settled gently over her: a comforter, weighty yet light as feathers. She knew it was the Holy Spirit. *Do not fear*, she heard in her heart. *I am here.*

She pulled herself up. She called the police, and Daniel. She waited.

Soon after the burglary, Jane went to a large luncheon for congressional wives. She still felt the warmth of the Comforter and did something she hadn't done before. After lunch, she shared her story with the two women who had spoken. They wept with her. One gave Jane a card with God's words from Isaiah. "I will not forget you! See, I have engraved you on the palms of my hands."[3] On the card was a picture of a little girl, held secure in God's strong hand.

Had God forgotten her when she was raped? In her heart, Jane now saw Christ, somehow with her that terrible night. She knew He did not plan it. He hated its vile evil, despised its shame. Jane didn't understand why He had allowed it . . . but for the first time she knew He was with her in the midst of her pain. She saw Christ's face, wet with tears. She felt Him holding her tenderly, like her husband . . . yet infinitely stronger, loving her more than she had ever dared to dream, her name engraved on His hands on the Cross.

The second woman gave Jane a small stone. It was black, with one word painted in white. *First.*

"It's not that you'll never have fear again," the woman told Jane. "But you know who to take it to. God is your Rock, your Stronghold, your Comforter. Keep Him first."

Time went by. Jane looked up every Scripture she could find on fear. Every one she could find on joy. She and Daniel spurred one another on to put Him first. God put all kinds of women in Jane's path; she could see a woman's face and sense if she'd been raped or abused, if she was part of the unspoken fellowship of fear and pain.

She was able to talk with them, hold them, help them. And in all this, Jane somehow became more and more aware of God's forgiveness for her own sins; she felt more responsive to His grace. The result was like a waterfall unleashed, thundering on the hard place in her heart and breaking it into a million pieces. She knew God loved her. She knew she was clean, in Him.

Still, every once in a while—on the street, or at a sports event—she'd see a man about the size and shape of her attacker, and a burst of fear would flare inside.

Then a friend invited Jane to an event at an urban church downtown. It was followed by a special dinner designed to build Christ-based friendships across racial and cultural differences. She recoiled. *I'll go anywhere*, she thought. *Outer Mongolia. Just don't send me to the inner city.*

But she went. A group of pastors, black and white, led the proceedings. At dinner Jane found herself seated next to a huge, muscular African American man. His name was William, he told her. He was quite open with his story.

William had spent eight years in one notorious federal prison, then seven in another, where a believer had visited him. "He shared the love of Jesus with me," William told Jane. "I cried out and I asked God to forgive me. I received Christ. He told me that all of my sins were as far as the east is from the west, that they were forgiven. Forgiven!

"When I got out of prison, I came here. Now I work with inner-city kids who are heading down the wrong path. I tell them about the love of God. I show them there's another way to live. And they listen. They know I've been there."

Jane's heart clenched. People didn't serve fifteen years in prison for minor offenses. This guy could well have raped or killed someone. But suddenly, just as her old fear uncoiled like a snake, ready to strike, a verse from Scripture crushed its head. *If anyone is in Christ, he is a new creation*, she thought. *The old has gone. The new has come!* This man next to her was a brother. New.

Jane closed her eyes. To her absolute shock, she found herself thinking words she had never dreamed she might utter. "Lord," she prayed, "I forgive the man who raped me. And I will pray every day for the rest of my life that someone will tell him about Jesus and that I will spend eternity with him."

It was impossible—but a flood of peace flowed over her, washing away the last traces of the fear that has filled her for years. A few minutes later, the pastor leading the dinner asked everyone to stand and sing "Jesus Loves Me," and to please take hold of one another's hands. Jane reached for the ex-prisoner's palm without flinching. And then she held it firmly as they sang together, their voices blending in the night and rising up toward heaven: thanks to the One who had engraved their names on His own hands.

In the years that followed, William became a close friend of Jane's. She gave the eulogy at his funeral. She returned often to the inner city, working for racial reconciliation and to help the poor. She learned new heights of joy, new depths of forgiveness and love. She walked with other victims through their pain and helped them give their fear to the One they could depend on for healing and grace.

And she was able to say that what had been meant for evil that long, dark night in 1974, God has used for good—in her own life and in the lives of many hurting, broken women.[4]

What of Jane's own pain over the years? There was no instant healing. God's work in her was a long process, helped by the loved ones who came alongside to shoulder her burden. But, she says, every tear she shed is intimately known by Christ. In that she has comfort today—even as she looks ahead to that Day when there will be no more mourning or crying or pain or death, when the old order of things has passed away, and Christ will make all things new.[5]

A thimble of divine blood would have been sufficient to wash away our sins and bring that new day to pass. But God's grace is not thrifty. The blood from Christ's cross flowed like a fountain. It sprayed from His heart. It is extravagant grace ... a gift of such divine enormity that our only human response is what we might call extravagant gratitude, a welling spring of joy, worship, service ... and forgiveness as we've been forgiven, forgiveness that makes no earthly sense.

Now, one final story. Though this one is fiction, and familiar, it too gives a picture of how thankfulness for God's extraordinary grace can compel us every ordinary day for the rest of our lives.

In Victor Hugo's 1862 classic *Les Misérables*, a man named Jean Valjean has been imprisoned for nineteen years at hard labor, in horrific conditions, for stealing a loaf of bread. He has survived his imprisonment by stoking schemes of revenge. Finally, he is released. He finds a construction job. But at the end of the day he is given half wages because he's an ex-convict. His anger boils. Then he is taken in for the night by the Bishop of Digne, as godly a character as can be found in literature.

The bishop shares his soup, bread, and wine. Valjean notes the heavy silver serving spoon and cutlery; he marks where they are stored. He figures they are worth double what he earned in the pitiful prison wages of nineteen long years, time that the government stole from him. In the middle of the night he sneaks to the cupboard, pulls out the silver basket, and flees into the night.

The next morning the bishop is up at sunrise, working in his garden. His elderly sister, who keeps house for him, comes out of the cottage.

"Do you know where the silver basket is?" she asks in a panic.

"Yes," the bishop replies.

"God be praised!" she shouts. "I did not know what had become of it."

The bishop had just found the basket where it had been thrown into the flower bed. He hands it to his sister.

She nods and then sputters. "But there's nothing in it. Where's the silver?"

"Ah!" says the Bishop. "It's the silver, then, that troubles you. I don't know where that is."

"Good heavens!" she shrieks. "It's stolen! The man who came last night stole it!"[6]

Unruffled, the bishop comes in for breakfast. As they are rising from the table, there is a commotion at the door. A group of policemen drag in a wild-eyed Jean Valjean. They had noticed him "acting like a convict," arrested him, and found the bishop's silver.

The bishop approaches Valjean, who is full of fear, shame, and despair.

"Ah, there you are!" he says, smiling. "I'm glad to see you. But I gave you the candlesticks, too, which are silver like the rest and would bring two hundred francs. Why didn't you take them along with your cutlery?"

Jean Valjean stares at the bishop, astonished.

The bishop takes the heavy, silver candlesticks from the mantle, presses them into Valjean's hands, and tells the policemen to go. They reluctantly release their prisoner. After they leave, the bishop whispers to Valjean:

"Do not forget, ever, that you have promised to use this silver to become an honest man."

Valjean, dumbfounded, does not recall any such thing. But the bishop continues: "Jean Valjean, my brother, you no longer belong to evil, but to good. It is your soul I am buying for you. I withdraw it from dark thoughts and from the spirit of perdition, and I give it to God!"[7]

Valjean stumbles away. He wrestles all that day with this Christlike grace, unable to accept that he can accept it. But by three o'clock the following morning, he is kneeling on the bishop's front step in prayer, surrendering his life to the God he knows only by the bishop's gift.

Forever grateful for the canceled debt he could never pay back, Jean Valjean pays it forward for the rest of his life. He eventually becomes mayor of a nearby town, manages a factory to help the poor, saves the life of a farmer who hates him, protects the weak and helps the needy. Given the opportunity to exact revenge on the police inspector who has hounded him for years, he instead pardons him, and lets him go.

Sacrificially doing good for others flowed directly from Valjean's jaw-dropping experience of grace. He knew he deserved absolutely nothing but to be thrown back into his prison hellhole. But the good bishop paid a great price to buy his soul, declared him innocent, and gave him lavish gifts. The rest of Jean Valjean's story is about radical gratitude.

Given what *we* have received, what's the rest of our story?

NOTES

Chapter 2: Fountain of Life

1. See John 15, particularly verses 4–12.
2. 1 Thessalonians 5:16–18.
3. Colossians 3:15–17.
4. Philippians 4:4b–7.
5. Jonathan Edwards, *A Treatise Concerning Religious Affections* (1746), online edition by International Outreach, Inc., PO Box 1286, Ames, Iowa 50014, 79.
6. Read Romans 8:28–39.
7. *Religious Affections*, 12.

Chapter 3: Whispers in the Night

1. Sue Anne Pressley and David Cho, "For Victims' Families, Nothing Will Take Away the Pain, Despair," *The Washington Post* (October 25, 2002).
2. Daniel 3:16–18. See Daniel 3 for the whole story. I love the phrase here, "... but even if he does not." The three young men are a great example of what Jonathan Edwards called "gracious gratitude." Their hope was not based in any particular outcome, like being saved from the fire, though I'm sure that was their preference. Their hope was based in God's character: "He is able." And they knew that He would rescue them from Nebuchadnezzar one way or another, by life or by death.
3. Stacey Randall, "Met in the Stairwell."
4. Thornton Wilder, *Three Plays* (New York: Harper & Row, 1957), 100. *Our Town* was first performed in 1938.
5. For more about Rusty's story, see chapter 12 of Charles Colson and Ellen Vaughn's *Being the Body* (Nashville: W Publishing, 2003).
6. Hebrews 12:28–29.

Chapter 4: Be the One!

1. Leviticus 13:45–46.
2. Sura 14:7.
3. "Gratitude Theory," *The Osgood File*, CBS Radio Network (July 12, 2002 and December 19, 2001), citing a study by Dr. Michael McCullough, Southern Methodist University, and Dr. Robert Emmons, the University of California at Davis.
4. This quoted exercise is from a Web review of Alan Jones and John O'Neil's *Season of Grace: The Life-Giving Practice of Gratitude*. Similarly, the aptly named Ursula Goodenough, a professor of biology at Washington University and author of *The Sacred Depths of Nature*, says that there's no need for a founding source of the blessings for which we are grateful. There are two kinds of people, she says: "Some need for their meaning to have a meaning maker, and others of us don't." (Web interview with Robert Wright.)
5. For more about the Birdwells' work, see their website, *http://www.facethefire.org/*. I deeply appreciate Brian's willingness to meet with me and describe his ordeal.
6. This is from a daily devotional meditation (February 18, 2003) by the Pope's preacher, Father Raniero Cantalamessa, O.F.M. Cap.
7. See Romans 1; this is from verse 21.
8. Romans 1:24, 26, 28, and following.

Chapter 5: Undeniably Delivered

1. Adapted by permission from Colson and Vaughn's *Being the Body*. All rights reserved.
2. Moses Schulstein, Yiddish poet, (1911–91).

Chapter 6: My Way—or the High Way?

1. Henry Fairlie, *The Seven Deadly Sins Today* (Washington, DC: New Republic Books, 1978), 40.
2. Sarah Ban Breathnach, cited on "Simple Abundance Online, The Home of Comfort and Joy on the World Wide Web," *http://www.simpleabundance.com/excerpts.html*.

3. Heather Klassen, "What's Right for Me," *ProudParenting.com*.

4. "Martha's Fate: Guilty," *SupermarketGuru.com*.

5. Edwards, *Religious Affections*, 79.

6. Cited in "The Leading Edge," *Leadership Training* by P. Brian Rice (York, Pa.: LWCC).

7. Henri J. M. Nouwen, *In the Name of Jesus: Reflections on Christian Leadership* (New York: Crossroad, 1993), 38–39.

8. With his blunt good cheer, Martin Luther wrote, "Faith is not what some people think it is.... 'Faith is not enough,' they say. 'You must do good works, you must be pious to be saved.' They think that, when you hear the gospel, you start working, creating by your own strength a thankful heart which says, 'I believe.' ... Such confidence and knowledge of God's grace makes you happy, joyful and bold in your relationship to God and all creatures. The Holy Spirit makes this happen through faith. Because of it, you freely, willingly and joyfully do good to everyone, serve everyone, suffer all kinds of things, love and praise the God who has shown you such grace." From "An Introduction to St. Paul's Letter to the Romans," Luther's German Bible of 1522, by Martin Luther, 1483–1546, translated by Rev. Robert E. Smith from *Dr. Martin Luther's Vermischte Deutsche Schriften*. Johann K. Irmischer, ed., vol. 63 (Erlangen: Heyder and Zimmer, 1854), 124–25. [EA 63:124–125] August 1994.

Chapter 7: Getting Naked

1. 2 Corinthians 4:6.

2. Revelation 3:17–18.

3. Revelation 3:19.

4. C. S. Lewis, *Of Other Worlds: Essays and Stories* (New York: Harcourt Brace Jovanovich, 1966).

5. Isaiah 32:9, 11 NASB.

6. From Jeremiah 5:7–11.

7. Hebrews 12:1 NLT.

8. C. S. Lewis, *The Voyage of the Dawn Treader* (New York: Macmillan, 1952), 88–91.

9. Oswald Chambers, *My Utmost for His Highest* (New York: Dodd, Mead, 1935), 282, October 8 entry.

Chapter 8: Out of Bounds

1. The information in this chapter is from interviews I conducted with Father Jenco in Costa Rica in June 1989 and from his winsome 1995 book, *Bound to Forgive*, which is unfortunately now out of print.

Chapter 9: Letting Go

1. This account is also given in Corrie ten Boom's book *Tramp for the Lord* (Old Tappan, N.J.: Fleming H. Revell, 1974). It was originally published in *Guideposts Magazine* (copyright 1972 by Guideposts Associates, Inc., Carmel, New York).
2. Matthew 6:15.
3. See Luke 15:11–32.
4. See Leviticus 15:19–30.
5. Mark 5:21–34.
6. Luke 5:12–13.

Chapter 10: No Regrets

1. See Acts 2:38–39.
2. Acts 11:17.
3. Acts 11:18.
4. From Luther's letter to John Staupitz in defense of his *Ninety-Five Theses*, cited by Jim Elder, Metanoia Ministries website, *www.metanoiaministries.org*.
5. See Luke 19:1–10.
6. Charles Dickens, *A Christmas Carol* (New York: Bantam 1965, 1986, 2002; first published in 1843), 79, 80.
7. See 2 Corinthians 7:8–10.
8. See 1 John 1:8–10.
9. Psalm 51:10.
10. Ezekiel 36:25–26.
11. This story and its quotes are from Christine C. Lawrence, "The Mystery of the Rain Forest Rash: She Wanted to Know What She'd Picked Up on Vacation . . . Until She Learned the Answer," *The Washington Post* (Tuesday, November 11, 2003), F1, F4.
12. From Psalm 32:3–4.
13. Matthew 3:8.
14. See Exodus 9:13–35.

Chapter 12: Remember

1. Remarks by the president at the Memorial Service in Honor of the STS-107 Crew, Space Shuttle Columbia, National Aeronautics and Space Administration, Lyndon B. Johnson Space Center, Houston, Texas, February 4, 2003.
2. From Genesis 3:1–6.
3. See Wendy Murray Zoba, "The Hidden Slavery," *Christianity Today* (November 2003).
4. Ibid., citing Kevin Bales, *Disposable People*.
5. These descriptions are influenced by the first chapter of Robert Massie's *Nicholas and Alexandra* (New York: Atheneum, 1967).
6. KR's journal entries are excerpted from Andrei Maylunas and Sergei Mironenko, *A Lifelong Passion: Nicholas and Alexandra, Their Own Story*, trans. Darya Galy (New York: Doubleday, 1997).
7. His name has been changed; he was part of Prison Fellowship's InnerChange Freedom Initiative.
8. See John 8:32.
9. The great paradox is that we can only be truly free when we make ourselves slaves to Christ. "Do you not know that when you present yourselves to someone as slaves for obedience, you are slaves of the one whom you obey, either of sin resulting in death, or of obedience resulting in righteousness? But thanks be to God that though you were slaves to sin, you became obedient from the heart to that form of teaching to which you were committed, and having been freed from sin, you became slaves to righteousness" (Romans 6:16–18 NASB).
10. Exodus 13:3 NASB.
11. See Deuteronomy 8.
12. See 1 Corinthians 11.24–25 NASB.
13. Oswald Chambers, *My Utmost for His Highest* (November 25 and 26).
14. Psalm 107:2 NASB.

Chapter 13: Out of the Blue

1. Elisabeth Elliott, *Through Gates of Splendor*, 40th Anniversary Edition (Wheaton, Ill.: Tyndale, 1996), pages 271–72 (Epilogue 2, January 1996).

Chapter 14: Forget

1. 1 John 1:9.
2. From Jeremiah 31:33–34.
3. Isaiah 43:25.
4. Hebrews 8:12 NASB.
5. The most extraordinary example of this is the Old Testament book of Hosea. In it, God forgives and tenderly restores His people from their shame, pictured through the prophet Hosea actually wooing back and restoring an adulterous wife.
6. Isaiah 54:4 NASB. Also see Isaiah 61:7:

   > Instead of their shame
   >   my people will receive a double portion,
   > and instead of disgrace
   >   they will rejoice in their inheritance;
   > and so they will inherit a double portion in their land,
   >   and everlasting joy will be theirs.
7. 1 Corinthians 15:9 NASB.
8. 1 Corinthians 15:10 NASB.
9. From Philippians 3:4–14.

Chapter 15: Look Up: The Grandeur of God

1. Isaiah 6:1–11.
2. See Philippians 3:4–10.
3. From Lawrence Martin Jenco, OSM, *Bound to Forgive: The Pilgrimage to Reconciliation of a Beirut Hostage* (Notre Dame, Ind.: Ave Maria, 1995), 49–50.
4. Gerard Manley Hopkins, "God's Grandeur."
5. Ken Ringle, *The Washington Post* (Tuesday, September 16, 2003), C-1.
6. See Ezekiel 1 for this account.

Chapter 16: Grieving, But Still Giving Thanks

1. This chapter is based on interviews with Bob Meyers in the spring of 2004. I am deeply grateful for his candor and model of Christian character.
2. Quoted in *The Virginian-Pilot* by Earl Swift, (October 12, 2003), A1.
3. Ibid.

4. Descriptions of Dean Meyers's death come from Sari Horwitz and Michael E. Ruane, *Sniper: Inside the Hunt for the Killers Who Terrorized the Nation* (New York: Random House, 2003), 127–33.
5. Transcript from *Larry King Live*, CNN (October 28, 2002).
6. Horwitz and Ruane, *Sniper*, 129.
7. Isaiah 55:9.

Chapter 17: Look Around: Circle of Friends

1. From Irina Ratushinskaya, *Pencil Letter* (New York: Knopf, 1988). Used by permission of Alfred A. Knopf, a division of Random House, Inc.
2. As the few examples in this chapter show, God is changing needy people's lives through the ministries of Romanian Christian Enterprises. For more about RCE, check out their website, *http://www.rcenterprises.org*.

Chapter 18: The Domain of Drudgery

1. Oswald Chambers, *My Utmost for His Highest* (New York: Dodd, Mead, 1935), 167, June 15 entry.

Chapter 19: Memory Rocks

1. See 1 Samuel 7:7–17.
2. See Joshua 3:9–4:24.
3. Joshua 4:23–24.
4. Genesis 49:24; Psalm 19:14; Isaiah 26:4; Isaiah 51:1.

Chapter 20: "Good Night and God Bless"

1. I deeply appreciate Paul Galanti's willingness to share his story. This chapter is based on interviews conducted in late 2003 and early 2004.

Chapter 22: Pleasures du Jour

1. Marcel Proust, quoted in Alice Flaherty, *The Midnight Disease* (New York: Houghton Mifflin, 2004).
2. Russell Cronkhite, *A Return to Sunday Dinner* (Sisters, Ore.: Multnomah, 2003), 6.
3. John Piper, *Don't Waste Your Life* (Wheaton, Ill.: Crossway, 2003), 19–20.
4. Psalm 115:8.
5. Psalm 98:4; Psalm 34:8; Isaiah 55:1; John 4:14a.

Chapter 24: Go!

1. Matthew 28:18–20.
2. Gregg Easterbrook, *The Progress Paradox: How Life Gets Better While People Feel Worse* (New York: Random House, 2003).
3. Robert J. Samuelson, "The Afflictions of Affluence," *Newsweek* (March 22, 2004), 45.
4. Ibid.
5. Ibid.
6. See Easterbrook, *The Progress Paradox*.
7. G. K. Chesterton, *A Utopia of Usurers, Collected Works*, Vol. V (San Francisco: Ignatius Press, 1987), 396.

Chapter 25: The Rest of the Story: Extravagant Gratitude

1. Luke 7:36–50.
2. Dan Allender, *Bold Love* (Colorado Springs: Navpress, 1993).
3. Isaiah 49:15b–16a.
4. Jane's story is based on interviews conducted in the spring of 2004. I admire her courage; her hope is that sharing her story here might give hope to others.
5. Revelation 21:4–5.
6. The dialogue in this exchange is from Victor Hugo, *Les Misérables*, trans. Lee Fahnestock and Norman MacAfee, based on the C. E. Wilbour translation (New York: Signet, 1987), 103.
7. Ibid., page 106.

We want to hear from you. Please send your comments about this book to us in care of zreview@zondervan.com. Thank you.

GRAND RAPIDS, MICHIGAN 49530 USA

WWW.ZONDERVAN.COM